For more cowgirl stories go to:
www.CowgirlSmarts.com

Published by: Reid Smith & Associates, Inc.
For reprint permission contact Ellen Reid
Smith at: www.ReidSmith.com or
www.CowgirlSmarts.com

Printed and bound on acid free paper
in the U.S.A.
Revised Edition 2007   10 9 8 7 6 5 4 3 2
First Printing 2004   10 9 8 7 6

ISBN 0-9760805-0-8

Stocking/Shelving Guide:
1. Women--Motivational
2. U.S. History--Western U.S.

This publication is designed to provide
accurate and authoritative information with
regard to the subject matter covered. It is
sold with the understanding that the author
and publisher are not engaged in rendering
professional advice. If advice or other expert
assistance is required, the services of a
competent professional person should be
sought.

COWGIRL SMARTS

How to Rope a Kick-Ass Life

Life Lessons From
Cowgirls Who Settled the West

by
Ellen Reid Smith

To Josef
You're the best pardner a
cowgirl could ever hope for.

Contents

Acknowledgements

Many thanks to my husband Josef who stoked my literary campfire, read more "chick lit" than he cares to admit and tirelessly helped me comb through historical documents in libraries and museums across the West. I couldn't have done it without you.

A big thank you also goes out to editor Susie Flatau and graphic designer Cheryl Rae who patiently worked with me in the final days of prepress crazies.

Thanks to Ann Parilla who knew when to give me a good swift kick or two. Every cowgirl should be lucky enough to have a friend like you.

I'd like to thank the following institutions and their librarians who helped me research my cowgirl heroes.

American Heritage Center
Austin Public Library
Bozeman Trail Museum
Buffalo Bill Historical Center
Buffalo Public Library
Carbon County Historical Society
Denver Public Library
Don King Western Museum
Jackson Hole Historical Society
Jim Gatchell Museum
Library of Congress
Montana Historical Society

Museum of New Mexico
Museum of the Rockies
Museum of Women's History, Billings
National Cowboy and Western Heritage Museum
National Cowgirl Museum and Hall of Fame
National Women's History Museum
Peaks to Plains Museum
Pioneer Women Museum
Powell Public Library
Santa Fe Trail Association
Texas Historical Commission
Texas State Historical Association
University of Oklahoma Western History Collections
Western Folk Life Center
The Western Trails Project
Wyoming State Historical Society
Yellowstone Gateway Museum

Preface

When I was a young girl, my dad always said, "Pumpkin, you can be anything you want to be." While I never understood why anyone would call a girl pumpkin, I did understand that being a woman wouldn't prevent me from taking a man's job—or at least it shouldn't. My dad always wanted me to be an electrical engineer—just like him. Luckily, my calculus skills put an early end to my studies as an engineer.

Going to a women's college drove the feminist message home even harder for me. However, I began to take it all for granted. While my professors were all singing Helen Reddy's "I Am Woman," I was more likely to be found singing Madonna's "Like a Virgin." I had come to believe that I could achieve anything, because the world would accept me as I was—a nauseatingly preppy girl in lime green skirts emblazoned with big frogs. Through dress alone, my roommates and I could have derailed the entire women's movement in one fell swoop. Sometimes naiveté is a great gift.

For years I believed I could easily become anything or anyone I wanted to be. But after graduation from college, I soon came face-to-face with the real world. I found only a handful of women in senior management, even fewer women scientists leading breakthrough research, a smattering of women in elected positions and no women CEOs in major companies. Where were my gutsy women role models? Where were my mentors? Where were the women who brought home the bacon and fried it up in a pan like Helen Ready told us?

With few female role models in my working world, I turned to history. Cowgirls from the Wild West became my role models. Stories about nineteenth-century cowgirls like Lucille Mulhall, Bertha Blancett and Fanny Seabride became my bedtime reading. Though they had been dead for longer than I had been alive, these cowgirls inspired and directed me. Don't get me wrong, I wasn't rounding up ghosts with western séances—though the concept is intriguing. Nope, I was solving my career and business problems by asking myself, "What would my cowgirl heroines do in my situation?" I began to think like a cowgirl, make decisions like a cowgirl and set big goals like a cowgirl. I had no intention of taking up rodeoing or cowboying as a profession, but I did want their cowgirl state of mind. I wanted to emulate their cowgirl smarts.

There's really no better role model for women than Wild West cowgirls. Even in their own time they were inspirational to corset-cinched women everywhere. Cowgirls showed a nation of women the right way to buck the norms to get what you want. They scoffed at Victorian vanity, demureness and social taboos. Their skin was tan, they boldly wore split skirts to ride and they mounted their ponies astride like any sensible cowhand. If you think bra burning was big in

6

the 1960s, you should have seen these cowgirls torch their side saddles. They proved that just like horses, rules are better when broken.

I knew these cowgirls could teach me a thing or two about how to dream big and make my dreams a reality. But I found that it takes a bushel of gumption, a dauntless attitude and years of learning to become cowgirl smart. With the help of these cowgirls, I've continued to develop my own cowgirl smarts and it has led to what many would call a kick-ass life.

My inspiration for writing Cowgirl Smarts came from a visit to the Cowgirl Hall of Fame in Fort Worth, Texas. There I entered the dark theater of the museum with thirty or forty other women to watch the museum's film on cowgirl spirit. I was taken aback by how much that film moved me. Its message was that all women have a cowgirl spirit, bucking to get out. It claimed you were just as likely to see the cowgirl spirit in a boardroom or art studio as on a ranch. Women all share the longing for the spirit of freedom and independence, but we each manifest it differently in our chosen work and play. The movie's message really hit home for me. As the lights came up, I was at first embarrassed to wipe a tear from my eye, only to see that half the women in the room were doing the same. At that point, I realized I wasn't alone, that many women aspire to find their cowgirl spirit, whether it is on golf course, running for a political office or volunteering for the Peace Corps. It was at that moment I was inspired to write *Cowgirl Smarts* and document the Cowgirl Creed for cowgirls and city slickers everywhere. I wanted to share what I had learned from my cowgirl heroines.

This book is designed to help women of all ages find their cowgirl spirit and develop their own cowgirl smarts by reading about the lives of some of my favorite cowgirls. To document these cowgirl stories, I spent years traveling the Western United States, visiting museums, libraries and historical societies researching the lives of my favorite cowgirls and collecting new stories about amazing cowgirls of whom few have ever heard. From my research, I identified key characteristics that successful cowgirls have in common and wrote what I call The Cowgirl Creed which encapsulates both these successful cowgirl characteristics and the unwritten rules that cowgirls have lived by for over 100 years. I then organized stories about some of the most remarkable cowgirls into the seventeen chapters of this book which are conveniently identical to the Cowgirl Creed.

The Cowgirl Creed
1. Dare to be a cowgirl
2. Buck the rules
3. Stay balanced in the saddle
4. Ride the trail of adventure
5. Dream as big as Texas
6. Be tough, but be feminine
7. Attack life like it's a 1,000 lb. steer
8. Saddle your own horse

9. Rein in your fears
10. Dress for success—the cowgirl way
11. Ride high in the saddle
12. Ride high, but stay grounded
13. Give others a leg up
14. Always get back on the horse
15. Ride beside your man
16. Recharge your cowgirl spirit
17. Die with your boots on

It's my belief that living the Cowgirl Creed is fundamental to becoming cowgirl smart. So each chapter of *Cowgirl Smarts* explains a principle of the Cowgirl Creed by sharing stories about remarkable cowgirls who exemplify that principle. At the end of each chapter you'll find ideas for putting the Cowgirl Creed into action. After reading a chapter or two, you'll think these cowgirl stories are audacious and amazing, but what's really remarkable is that they are all true.

With these lessons under your belt buckle, any cowgirl or city slicker can become cowgirl smart. After all, cowgirl smarts is a state of mind, not a state of horse. So let 'er buck!

Introduction

When writing about the Wild West, both historians and Hollywood left out the cowgirl. Many historians would have you believe that pioneering women all stayed home, close to their tea sets. (It's my guess that most sold their tea sets in exchange for a good horse.) One of the toughest chores that Hollywood had for Dale Evans was riding to the café for sandwiches. You can bet that Dale never asked Roy to fetch some sandwiches. The truth is, that women cowboyed on ranches all over the West during the early 1800s. They took on the same chores as men and when they earned their spurs, they were accepted as cowboy equals.

The same was true for women in rodeo. Historians would have you believe that women didn't rope steers or ride broncs until the 1900s, when in fact many women were competing informally against neighbors in local ranch rodeos in the 1800s. Records indicate that by 1887 Buffalo Bill was adding women to his Wild West shows as fast as he could scout the female talent. It seems the public had an appetite for feminine women performing daring western stunts.

From the Wild West shows, dozens of talented cowgirls went into professional rodeo and were frequently allowed to compete against men. Cowgirls excelled at all rodeo events until the late 1940s, when women's events were cut in order to increase the purse for men (Some things never change!). When cowgirls were reduced to competing for rodeo queen and best barrel racer, they did what you'd expect of any gutsy, independent woman—they started the All-Girl Rodeo in 1947. This organization later became the WPRA (Women's Professional Rodeo Association) and it is the oldest women's professional sports association in the world. Leave it to cowgirls to blaze their own trails.

Despite the many factual accounts of cowgirls across the West, the general public can only recall the names of western bad girls. Cattle thieves and murderers like Belle Star and Sally Skull have been made into western heroines. Stories about women like Etta Place, who robbed banks with the Sundance Kid, have received more press time than all the real cowgirl heroes combined. To the casual observer of history, cathouse madams with their bevy of shady ladies were the only women earning their own way. It makes me spittin' mad, because it's just not true.

Stories of infamous wild-bunch women have been elevated to that of legends, while the cowgirl stands quietly in the background. It's an injustice that the real cowgirl heroes of the West—women who settled the land, who earned women the right to vote and who blazed the trail and set standards for the new Americana woman—always get second billing to women outlaws. Well this book is intended to change that.

When people think of real cowgirls in the Wild West, the words gutsy, tough, hardworking and honest come to mind. People remember how cowgirls had to buck all societal norms just to be cowgirls. Hell, putting on pants or riding astride could get them put in jail, run out of town or—least of all—scorned. These cowgirls weren't just tough, they were ballsy. They didn't give a rat's tail what others thought of them because they were pursuing their dreams of being cowgirls. They showed women everywhere how to make their dreams of freedom come true—freedom from the confinements of Victorian society and the feel of freedom while riding full gallop through wide open spaces. Cowgirls knew that from the back of a horse, the world looked wider. And because cowgirls were a generous bunch, they were kind enough to take their eastern sisters along for the ride of their lives.

Some cowgirls in the Wild West were debutante runaways, whose daddies spent thousands of dollars trying to bring them back home. But most were unlettered women full of wisdom beyond their years. While a formal education might keep a cowgirl's mind entertained, it wouldn't help her bring in the cattle, settle a spooked horse or fight off a mountain lion. Cowgirls lived by the seat of their pants, that is, when they were allowed to wear them. The best measure of any situation was usually their common sense. There was no guide book titled, "How to Tame the West" at the library—heck, there weren't even any libraries. What these cowgirls had was cowgirl smarts. They lived by an un-written Cowgirl Creed that helped them tame the West and rope a kick-ass life. The trouble is, no one bothered to write it down. The Cowgirl Creed has been handed down from mother to daughter for generations, until it's become an intrinsic component of ranch culture.

Until *Cowgirl Smarts* was published, about the closest thing to a written Cowgirl Creed was at the National Cowgirl Museum and Hall of Fame in Fort Worth, Texas. High up in the rotunda, the museum's designers decorated the walls with what they call "Cowgirl Spirit Words." They include:

Genuine	Authentic
Confident	Determined
Original	Independent
Dependable	Dauntless
Adventurous	Dedicated
A good hand	Visionary
Celebrated	Earnest
Skillful	Passionate
Clever	Focused
Spirited	Honored
Bold	Resourceful
True	Respected
Steadfast	Fearless
Hardworking	Trustworthy

Used with permission from the National Cowgirl Museum and Hall of Fame

These spirit words are characteristics

to which all cowgirls aspire. But upon closer examination, you'll see that these aren't just cowgirl characteristics, they are characteristics all women would like to have—for themselves, their daughters and their sons. But while these words describe some of the most famous cowgirls, they don't convey the cowgirl lessons that women have been passing from one generation to the next. They don't explain the unwritten Cowgirl Creed that cowgirls have been living by for over 100 years. These cowgirl lessons that make up the Cowgirl Creed needed to be documented, so here they are:

The Cowgirl Creed

1. Dare to be a cowgirl
2. Buck the rules
3. Stay balanced in the saddle
4. Ride the trail of adventure
5. Dream as big as Texas
6. Be tough, but be feminine
7. Attack life like it's a 1,000 lb. steer
8. Saddle your own horse
9. Rein in your fears
10. Dress for success   the cowgirl way
11. Ride high in the saddle
12. Ride high, but stay grounded
13. Give others a leg up
14. Always get back on the horse
15. Ride beside your man
16. Recharge your cowgirl spirit
17. Die with your boots on

The Cowgirl Creed may sound a bit horsy with all the riding and roping metaphors, but it truly is adaptable by all women in any environment. The Cowgirl Creed is a code for living a more fulfilled life. It's appropriate for teens, mothers and women in their twilight years, because the concepts can be applied at any age or any stage of life.

So grab your hat and pull on your boots, because the Cowgirl Creed is designed to inspire you to cowgirl up and rope a kick-ass life.

Author's Note

To write this book, I researched thousands of pages in books, newspapers, magazines, journals and recorded oral histories. When facts and events didn't match, I dug deeper in an effort to always present the most correct versions. I'm sure there are historians who will argue with some of the dates because few historians agree on when the first woman rode in a rodeo or when the first woman branded her own cattle. This is because the history of women in the West has been taken from women's diaries which by their very nature are inconsistent.

I greatly admire the cowgirls in this book and though I have chosen in some places to skip their minor shortcomings, I've never exaggerated their stories. These cowgirls' stories are amazing because they are true.

1. Dare to Be a Cowgirl

As every cowgirl knows, when you're on horseback an established trail isn't necessarily the best, the quickest or the most rewarding route. However, blazing your own path can be difficult. When cowgirls in the 1800s dared to ride the road less traveled, they faced numerous challenges. To begin with, cowgirls were so rare that the term "cowgirl" hadn't even been coined. Cowgirls were first called "cowboy-girls."

In many states, like Texas, cowgirls found it difficult to establish ranches because women weren't allowed to own land or buy and sell cattle. However, there was one woman who cleverly broke all the rules to become a rancher, because she dared to be cowgirl. She registered her own brand when it was unthinkable and rode the cattle trails when others said she couldn't. She eventually became one of the wealthiest cattlewomen in Texas—earning her the title of Texas Cattle Queen. Her name was Elizabeth Johnson Williams.

Lizzie, as she was called, was born in 1840 in Missouri, the second of seven children. Her father moved the family to Texas, teaching in three towns before settling in Hays County and establishing The Johnson Institute. Following in her father's footsteps, Lizzie attended The Johnson Institute and earned a degree in 1859 from Chappell Hill Female College. She taught in her father's school before founding her own primary school in Austin, Texas.

From all accounts, Elizabeth Johnson seemed a typical, demure school teacher, teaching French, math and bookkeeping. But the real Lizzie Johnson was quietly becoming a cowgirl. To supplement her teaching income, Lizzie kept books for cattlemen, which taught her about the cattle business. For extra money, she wrote articles about ranching under a nom de plume, since in the 1860s, women weren't supposed to know anything about ranching. Keeping books for successful cattlemen not only alerted her to the profits in ranching, but also served as a valuable education in buying and selling cattle.

With the money she saved from writing and teaching, she invested $2,500 in a Chicago cattle company that she learned about through her cattlemen clients. The investment paid her 100% in dividends for three straight years until she sold it for $20,000. Using her cowgirl smarts, Lizzie remained cloaked as a school teacher, while quietly becoming a shrewd cattlewoman.

In 1871, Lizzie became one of the first women in Texas to register her own cattle brand. She bought approximately ten acres of land in Austin and quietly began acquiring a small herd of cattle that she branded herself. Over the next eight years, Lizzie grew her herd, frequently buying and selling cattle under a man's name. The Civil War left a serious manpower shortage in Texas, and without fences, unbranded cattle were plentiful for cowboys who were skilled at brush popping (charging into thick brush to drive the cattle out). Lizzie was an accomplished brush popper and she frequently used this talent to roundup unbranded cattle as a way to expand her cattle holdings.

Though Lizzie was becoming a tough and shrewd cowgirl, she still had a penchant for fashion. With her cattle earnings, she took a trip to New York and filled her closet with the latest fashions—which included $10,000 in diamonds. In the 1800s that was some serious "bling, bling." While Lizzie was known to wear velvet and diamonds in town, she was all business in calico and bonnets on the ranch. Over time, she dared to let her cowgirl spirit show, sometimes acting more like a cattleman than a lady. On the streets in Austin, Lizzie would call out to her cattlemen friends, "Hello, you old cattle thief!" As an avid brander of stray cattle, she knew she was the pot calling the kettle black. She was an incorrigible cowgirl cut-up.

For years, Lizzie had been too busy managing her cattle holdings to marry. Austinites thought her independent nature would never attract a man, but at age thirty-six she married a prominent businessman and preacher by the name of Hezekiah G. Williams. Sometimes he was a successful preacher, but rarely was he a successful businessman. Some say he couldn't find a cow with a bell around its neck in a round pen.

Before their marriage in 1879, Lizzie made her husband-to-be sign a prenuptial agreement.

All property, cattle and future profits were to stay in their separate names. Not only did Lizzie dare to be a cowgirl, she dared to insist on having one of the first prenuptial agreements in Texas initiated by a woman. As it turns out, that was one cowgirl smart move, for Lizzie had to bail her husband out of several bad business ventures. Trying to teach her husband to be a better businessman, she called these bailouts "loans" and made him pay back every cent.

Between 1879 and 1889, Lizzie became the first woman to drive her own herd up the Chisholm Trail. Though a lady in the city, she was 100% cowgirl on the trail. She was as tough as any cowhand and a shrewd buyer of livestock. When she and Hezekiah went to the cattle sale pens, she'd insist the cowhands put the best steers in her herd. She was also known to instruct the cowhands to round up any unbranded calves from her husband's herd and quickly apply her own brand. When driving cattle, Lizzie would ride alongside her hired cowhands while her "soft" husband rode in a buggy at a safe distance.

Given the harsh terms by which she dealt with her husband, many thought she didn't truly love him, but that couldn't have been more wrong. When Lizzie's husband died in 1914, she bought a $600 coffin—a huge amount in those days. When she sent payment for the coffin to the funeral home, she attached a note which read, "I loved the old buzzard this much."

With her husband gone, Lizzie became a

recluse. Her net worth was in excess of $250,000 that included real estate holdings in six counties, but she lived the last years of her life in a small one-room apartment in the basement of a building in Austin. When she died in 1923, she was one of the wealthiest cattle queens in the state. Daring to be a cowgirl had been a very lucrative decision for Lizzie, but I know that she must have valued the adventure of being a cowgirl more than the money, because after her death, they found over $2,500 poorly hidden in Lizzie's house and a fortune in diamonds in an unlocked box, but her mementos from trail drives, love notes from her husband and a feather from her pet birt were kept under lock and key. Sure she loved to make money, but she never lost sight of what made life truly rich: living the cowgirl life and sharing it with those you love.

Lizzie dared to be a cowgirl and in return, she lived a kick-ass life.

Lessons Learned

Lizzie was the embodiment of an idea whose time had not yet come—she was emancipated in every sense of the word. By telling Lizzie's story, I'm not proposing that to be cowgirl smart you must dare to be a real cowgirl. But I am proposing that you dare to think like one. Women can learn some important lessons from Lizzie's bold, horsy lifestyle. She used her cowgirl smarts to find her passion in life and followed that passion even when it was seemingly off limits to women. She could have continued with her safe job as a school teacher and an owner of a profitable school. But because she dared to be a cowgirl, she went on to live a fuller and richer life.

Lizzie's story makes another important point. When you're forced to work within rules you cannot change, employ cleverness and learn to work around them. Lizzie was forced to work under Victorian notions that women shouldn't be ranchers—a dilemma that made buying, selling and trailing her cattle difficult. But she didn't sit and whine about it; she acknowledged that life wasn't fair, and then she outsmarted the bad and rolled with the good. Now that's cowgirl smart!

Here are some ideas for thinking about how you would dare to live your life like a cowgirl—that is, on your own terms:

1. Evaluate your life. Make a list itemizing what you like and don't like about your life. What aspects do you dare change? Use your cowgirl smarts to change things within your control and to cleverly work around that which you cannot. The ride of life should be down the trail of your own choosing.

2. Dare to change. If you're saddled with a job that's comfortable but not fulfilling, you need to find a new trail to ride. Remember that the paved path is not always the quickest or most fulfilling. While the rugged path is often more challenging, it is infinitely more rewarding. Find a new trail and kick up some dust!

3. Know your options and study your trail map. Don't just look before you leap, research the influencing factors before making a life change. Lizzie may have been a daring cowgirl, but she always scouted the trail and carried a reliable trail map. Follow her lead and scout the best trail for you.

4. Ride beside a cowgirl, if only for a day. Find a clever woman with your same passion or someone who makes the stay-at-home mom job look exciting. Ask if you can ride alongside her for a few days. I've done this many times. It's easier than you think to find a generous cowgirl. Simply find a leader in your chosen path and call her up to ask for advice. Come on, I dare you!

2. Buck the Rules

In the 1800s, it was considered terribly unfeminine for women to fill jobs typically held by cowboys. But many cowgirls, out of a sense of duty and to feed their families, punched cows and broke horses on their family ranch. They held their own against the cowboys. Some of these women were left at home for weeks to break the colts while the men rode the range—thus some women became bronc riders out of necessity. For other cowgirls, riding broncs and competing in rodeos fulfilled lifelong dreams. The competition, camaraderie and road trips filled with adventure helped them rope more out of life.

Let's face it, men knew that women who competed in rodeo's were a spectacle in the 1800s and early 1900s and rodeo producers made thousands of dollars putting women in their sensational Wild West shows. Respectable Victorian ladies did not make a spectacle of themselves in the show ring, because it was considered an unwholesome passion for what many saw as a solely male activity. But while some people ridiculed these women for pursuing their cowgirl dreams, crowds loved the cowgirls' wild daring, their verve and their romantic beauty. The only thing comparable in the 21st Century is female wrestlers on TV—you want to look away, but the novelty and their athleticism keeps you glued to the tube in weird fascination.

Colonel Gordon Lillie, better known as Pawnee Bill, was one of the more famous producers of Wild West shows in the late 19th and early 20th centuries. He had a different way of looking at life, particularly when it came to women. He knew there was no such thing as a *normal* job when hiring and promoting women. The women in his shows broke all the rules of Victorian society by competing against men, riding wild animals and participating in rough-rider shoot outs. He knew that taking women out of normal roles was what sold tickets.

Pawnee Bill's Historic Wild West shows played to a sense of daring and adventure in men and women everywhere. He had a penchant for strong women, so you can imagine how strong a woman Pawnee Bill wanted in a bride. He found that strength in woman named May Lillie.

May was the Wild West's champion of making women more confident and helping them lasso more out of life. May once said, "Let any normally healthy woman who is ordinarily strong, screw up her courage and tackle a bucking bronco, and she will find the most fascinating pastime in the field of feminine athletic endeavor—there is nothing to compare, to increase the joy of living. Once accomplished, she'll have more real fun than any pink tea or theater party or ballroom ever yielded." May Lillie knew how to rope a kick-ass life by bucking all the rules.

Bertha Kaepernick Blancett rode in Pawnee Bill and May's Wild West show for several years. But Bertha was one contentious cowgirl that that May didn't have to encourage. Bertha was a smart, hard driving cowgirl who managed to buck the rules all by herself. For years, Bertha had petitioned to enter the bronc riding contests at some of the biggest rodeos in the U.S., but was never allowed to compete with the men. In 1897, at Cheyenne's Frontier Days (the granddaddy of all rodeos), Bertha's luck finally changed.

On that fateful day in 1897, the sky poured buckets and completely mucked-up the arena. There's nothing like mud made of dirt and horse manure to make you think twice about being thrown from a bronc. The cowboys didn't want their boots landing in this muck, much less their faces. Wouldn't you know it, those mealy-mouthed men refused to ride, leaving a grandstand of spectators disappointed. Men being men, they tried to encourage some of the women riders to put on an exposition of bronc riding. The men thought the thousands of rodeo attendees would think women covered in mud would be just as entertaining as cowboys on wild horses and they'd be able to keep the ticket sales. They were right and all stayed to watch the women fall into the mud. What is it with men's fascination with women covered in mud? Some things never change.

Though they crowd anxiously stayed to watch women mud slingers, they saw a show of a very different kind. Bertha saw her opportunity and grabbed it by the horns. She put those men to shame. Bertha's bronc ride was supposed to be an exposition ride ending in a good mud bath, but Bertha rode that bronc like a tornado and landed like a princess. Practically taming the horse, she rode it to submission and finished with a perfect dismount. Her score was so good the men decided they'd better ride lest they be judged as lame as a calf in a mud hole. So the men rode out of shame and it was the women who enjoyed watching the men take a mud bath.

Bertha's ride was a huge success, but possibly too successful, because the men had their pride hurt. Consequently, it was several years before the Cheyenne officials let women compete at bronc riding again. Other rodeo producers weren't so short sighted. They knew women on wild horses who broke all the rules meant increased ticket sales so Bertha went on to compete in other rodeos throughout the West.

Though women had never done it before, Bertha bucked the rules and it opened the door not just for herself, but other women as well. Once cowgirl bronc riding caught on, Bertha found new rules to break by riding slick like the men. Riding slick meant she refused to ride with her stirrups hobbled or tied beneath the horse. Typically, women bronc riders rode with the stirrups hobbled for added leverage—though in retrospect, it was likely the cause of some serious injuries when women couldn't get their feet out of the stirrups. Riding slick made the ride easier, but the technique was not afforded most men.

30

Bertha's daring and perseverance truly paid off. She went on to win many bronc events against men in Australia and won all-round cowgirl at the Pendleton Round-Up every year from 1911 to 1918. Through her unstoppable perseverance and willingness to buck the rules, Bertha ensured women's bronc riding was a part of mainstream rodeo for some thirty-odd years. Thanks Bertha!

After WWII, men demanded larger rodeo winnings, so women's bronc riding was cut and women were no longer allowed to compete with men. Today, you'll have to check out the women's rodeo circuit (see the Women's Professional Rodeo Association at www.wpra.com) to see women on broncs. My hat is off to all the cowgirls of the WPRA who follow in Bertha's footsteps and dare to buck the rules. They are truly cowgirl smart.

Lessons Learned

Has your job application or promotion request been turned down again? Bertha's bronc riding applications were turned down for years before she got her big break. But did she give up? Hell no! She knew that rules, like horses, were meant to be broken. She knew that if she stayed in the saddle, she could change the world of rodeo forever—and she did.

Bertha's story also proves that just as in breaking or starting horses, patience and timing is everything. It wasn't just her strength and determination that gave her a break in life—she used what was under her ten gallon hat—cowgirl smarts. More prepared than any man, she waited behind the bucking shoots. When her opportunity came, she was ready to seize the moment. Some say Bertha was lucky to get her big break on that rainy afternoon in Cheyenne, but like most cowgirls, Bertha defined luck as the point when hard work meets opportunity.

Are you ready to seize the next big opening in your organization? Maybe you're waiting for the perfect location for your store to open up. Will you be ready?

Bertha's story could be yours. Let her inspire you to ask for opportunities where no woman has ridden before. Maybe you're just the cowgirl to bust the norms wide open by being the youngest woman ever to hold a coveted office or earn a meaningful award. The more often you buck the norms, the easier it will become. Here are a few ideas to get you started:

1. Adopt the courage of a cowgirl. Just because women haven't done it, doesn't mean you can't. Decide what you want in your life and your work, seize the moment and go for it at full gallop.

2. Adopt the motto of Laurel Thatcher Ulriech: "Well behaved women rarely make history." Think of all the women who were first to enter their profession or first in one achievement or another. Most were never described as "well behaved." Don't be afraid of what others think of your less stereotypical behavior.

2. When others tell you no, don't give up! If you're in a seemingly dead-end job, use your cowgirl smarts and wait for the right opportunity to show them all up. Beating politics in the working world is like roping calves—timing is everything. Watch for your opportunity and seize the moment!

3. Use rejection as fire for your fight! When you get knocked from your saddle, get back on the horse. Persistence has paid off for more than one cowgirl.

4. Take pride in not being normal. Who wrote the definition of normal anyway? You won't find any mention of women listed under "normal" in the dictionary. Why would you want an adjective like "normal" hanging around your neck. I sure don't! It's like bragging that you're "average." So buck the rules that you think "normal" women wouldn't dare break and you'll be glad when others tell you, "You're just not normal."

5. Find a mentor who is successful at breaking the rules and walk a mile in her boots. Whether it's a mother you admire or a woman in a position you'd like to fill, find a mentor and ask her how she broke the rules but still has seemingly perfect children or how she got promoted writing her own rule book. If women are the minority in your profession or organization, ask your mentor how she learned to ride in a man's world. Let your mentor know your ambitions and work together to break into the all-male rodeo in your organization.

3. Stay Balanced in the Saddle

Life is like riding balanced in the saddle—it requires a lot of practice to acquire and work to maintain. Once you find your balance, stirrups and a saddle become unnecessary for balance. Balanced riders look as though they move effortlessly with the horse. In actuality, staying balanced requires stability that comes from your inner core muscles. Riding through life is no different: your stability comes from your inner being. You can spot an unbalanced rider because she holds onto the saddle horn or pulls on the reins to steady herself. When our lives get out of balance, we do the same thing—we grasp for stability or ask too much of others.

Whether you're riding a horse or loping down the trail of life, you don't want to find yourself unbalanced and thrown from the saddle. You want to keep a balanced seat that will allow you to move in rhythm with life and keep you in control through the inevitable bucks and abrupt stops that life throws your way.

Women with cowgirl smarts find and maintain balance in their lives. Whether they are juggling work and play, eating and drinking in moderation, sharing responsibilities with their partners or ensuring time for themselves as well as their kids, they strive to achieve balance in their lives. But much like riding, everyone has a different point of equilibrium. What feels right for one rider may not work for another. That's because only you can define balance. If you're looking to other riders to find balance, you're merely copying their posture and that might not yield a balanced seat for you.

To live a kick-ass life you must define your own sense of balance. Your definition of balance will be the equilibrium between what you want to do and what you have to do. Adele von Ohl Parker was an eccentric cowgirl who lived a life mixing with high society and down and out circus performers. She had a passion for expensive horses and bawdy Vaudeville. Some outsiders thought that while Adele had uncanny balance on a horse, she had little to none in her life. In fact, many thought she had a loose screw or two. But her friends and students in North Olmstead, Ohio, knew otherwise. Adele chose a life of extremes that felt good to her.

To understand Adele and how she balanced extremes in her life, you need to look at her background. She was raised in New Jersey, by aristocratic parents who were successful horse breeders and trainers of fine riding stallions in a society that no longer valued horsepower. Her family began importing fine horses into the United States in 1682 and supplied valuable scout horses to George Washington during the American Revolution. Their horses were so respected that they were honored in the state seal of New Jersey, which features the head of a black stallion, said to be trained by the von Ohl family.

In 1902, Adele and her sister could be found using the finest stallions in New Jersey to plow the neighbors' fields to put food on the table. With money tight, Adele left home to become an actress. Though there isn't a record of Adele having any formal theatrical training, her acting debut in Plainfield, New Jersey was met with stunning reviews. *The Plainfield Courier-News* described Adele's performance as "a triumph, for almost every one of her long speeches was followed by a burst of hand clapping." Though she went on to be one of the highest paid actresses in New York, she found she was snubbed by the same society in which her parents once belonged. Actresses in her time were considered secondary citizens, regardless of whether their bloodline was aristocratic.

When Buffalo Bill's Wild West Show came to New York, Adele didn't hesitate to join a show that combined her love of riding with acting. With an unmatchable ability to train horses and perform daring equestrian feats, she quickly became one of the stars of Buffalo Bill's show.

In 1909, she married Jim Parker, who also rode in Buffalo Bill's shows. A year later, the two were starring in a new show called "Cheyenne Days." The show became one of the most successful international equestrian shows ever produced and they toured the globe together for five years. Part of Adele's success came from her ability to perform dangerous horse stunts like picking up gold coins from the arena floor while hanging from the side of a galloping horse.

Usually she scooped up the coin with her hand, but for theatrics, she'd pick the coin up with her teeth. She loved stallions with spirit and frequently rode on stage with her horse rearing. Such feats thrilled audiences, but terrified musicians in the orchestra pit since Adele didn't shy from jumping over the pit or even into it. She was a daring horsewoman, and the crowds loved her.

In 1915, when ticket sales for Wild West shows began to lag, Buffalo Bill and Adele parted ways, and Adele and her husband moved to Hollywood. Adele spent almost ten years as an actress, cowboy trainer and stuntwoman for "B" westerns. Many a "cowboy" stunt was actually performed by a cowgirl named Adele. She proved to them all that some of the best cowboys are girls.

While filming in California, Adele built a small barn on a back studio lot in Pasadena and in her spare time taught low-income kids to ride. She called them the Junior Rough Riders. Without proper schools to attend, these boys were illiterate. Adele ensured her students learned to read and do simple arithmetic in payment for their lessons. When asked why she taught children, she relayed a story about the time she was riding down a street in Los Angeles and a little girl walked up to her mare Daisy and asked Adele what it was. It was then she decided to teach city-slicker children the joy and discipline of horsemanship. Combining her love of horses and teaching children gave Adele the balance in life she had always needed.

They only thing that could drag Adele away from her Junior Rough Riders was a man's dream of taming wild horses. Adele followed her husband to Montana where they spent time rounding up wild horses. After years of performing dangerous stunts on horseback, it was probably the only ride that could still put goose bumps down their spines. But by 1929, their money grew short as did Adele's patience with her husband's unwillingness to leave Montana.

In 1929, Adele decided to take her own show on the road where she found limited success and much anguish producing and starring in a traveling show. With only seventy cents in her purse, she debarked the train in Cleveland, to find her booking cancelled. Not to be beaten, Adele used her cowgirl smarts to turn a catastrophe into an opportunity to return to what she loved most: teaching children to ride.. The fact that she arrived in Cleveland with seven horses and a rabbit to feed and only seventy cents to her name didn't faze Adele. She marched into the nearest soda shop with her pet rabbit and paid what few cents she had for a milkshake. She then called all the newspapers to report a thirsty giant rabbit in the soda shop drinking milkshakes from a straw. When reporters arrived, they found her well-trained rabbit politely sharing a milkshake with Adele. The reporters ate it up. The picture of Adele and her rabbit sharing a milkshake was priceless and it worked to gain publicity for her new Von Ohl School of Riding. Due to her successful publicity stunt, she was able to start a handful of students the next day and feed her treasured horses. Word spread of her student's success and she saved enough cash to purchase a small piece of land in North Olmsted just outside of Cleveland. She called it The Parker Ranch, but was later more likely to refer to her land as "Paradise." At Adele's ranch, kids learned as much about life as they did about riding.

On the Parker Ranch, it wasn't uncommon to see a group of Indians camping on the lawn, fifty goats from an animal rescue or cast-off circus elephants bathing in the river. She took in all the sick and broken animals that people brought her way. One student remembers entering her house on a cold winter day to find Adele painting a portrait of the donkey standing in her kitchen, while a dog, a cat, a pig and a fawn all slept side-by-side in front of the fire. Adele could work magic with animals.

The Parker Ranch became a gathering place not only for recovering animals, but also for performers spun off from failing Wild West shows, circuses and washed-up Hollywood careers. Trick ropers, clowns, bronc riders and horse trainers would converge on the ranch and throw impromptu shows to earn enough money to move onto the next town. When students arrived at the ranch, they never knew what to expect: Ms. von Ohl Parker in formal riding attire barking commands or a menagerie of performers with one foot in the poor house and the other in a stirrup. It might have seemed that Adele's life was "unbalanced," when in fact she had found her calling to help others.

Adele taught riding for a dollar a week and kept her wild child alive by ending each semester with a rowdy, Wild West show. It was a far cry from the $100 a week she made starring in Buffalo Bill's shows, or her fat Hollywood paychecks, but she reveled in the new balance she had created in her life using horses both to earn money and help others.

Other incidents led neighbors to think that Adele's life was completely out of balance. She'd give all her hay away to save the horses of a broke rancher, even though she had no idea how she'd refill her own hay barn. She'd loan her last fifty dollars to a laid-off cowboy, leaving no money for her own groceries. Somehow she always managed to survive: hay would be donated, friends would bring food or she'd find a buyer for a horse. Worrying about tomorrow wasn't how Adele lived life. She lived to keep performing, teaching and training horses. Her definition of balance was extreme: worry about the horses, the students and the show, and everything else would take care of itself.

Even Adele's house was extreme, but to her there was a balance between riding and housework—as long as she did as little as possible of the latter. With recovering animals in every corner of her house, you can imagine the dirt. Adele once insisted a friend have a cup of hot chocolate, but he very reluctantly accepted, knowing the cup was likely to have chili residue in the bottom. For her, keeping a balanced life didn't put housekeeping high on the list of important chores.

There is no doubt that Adele lived a life of extremes, but few who knew her well ever thought of her life as unbalanced. Amidst every dust storm blown her way, Adele had the uncanny ability to find a safe barn and turn it into her own paradise. She may have ridden to a very different beat than what others expected, but she always stayed balanced in the saddle of life.

Lessons Learned

I recently asked my seventy-four-year-old mother if she would do anything differently if she could live her life again. She quickly replied, "I would have cleaned house a little less and gotten out more." Adele's life may sound a bit out of balance to you, but I think women whose housekeeping leaves little time for anything else may be more unbalanced. I'm not proposing that having cowgirl smarts means having a dirty house or apartment, but to rope more out of life, you have to find a balance. That dirt on your car won't make it undrivable. The stain on your daughter's shirt doesn't mean you love her any less. Spending more time with family and less time at work may make it more difficult to balance your budget, but you will likely find your life to be more in balance.

Finding balance also means listening to the cowgirl spirit inside you. When your cowgirl spirit is bursting to get out of the stable, by all means open the door and go for a gallop. But listen just as closely to your more sensible side that knows when kids need a mother's arms or a business deadline has to be met. Women with cowgirl smarts listen to both voices in their head and find a balance that's as responsible as it is fulfilling.

If your cowgirl spirit isn't quite halter broke, you're probably having some trouble balancing the scale of life. Use your cowgirl smarts and develop a discipline to avoid always doing what you want to do, versus what you need to do. Slow down and take responsibility. Riding balanced in the saddle is easier to do at a trot than a gallop.

Here are a few ideas for staying balanced in the saddle:

1. Increase your fun quotient. Keep a diary for several weeks and track the time you spent doing things you truly love. When you tally up the time spent, what percentage of your waking hours does it represent? If the percentage isn't acceptable, reevaluate your "have-to-do" list. Would a cowgirl find these tasks critical? Another source of measurement is your date book or PDA. Are all the entries eat, work or sleep? If so, you need to cowgirl up and get a life.

2. Learn to make trade-offs. What would you sacrifice for a good adventure? How about buying fewer designer labels or mowing your own yard to save money. Would you babysit a friend's child one weekend this month so that you can take off a weekend next month? Finding time for an adventure could be as easy as not cleaning the house one week each month, or as difficult as finding a new job with more reasonable hours. Make trade-offs in return for a better, more balanced ride, you'll be glad you did.

3. Change your definition of clean. Whoever told you that the woman with the cleanest house wins, was wrong. Hygiene is important, but distinguish it from compulsive. If you find you're routinely putting off your family to clean house, you probably need a new definition of clean or need to find the cash to hire a maid.

4. Shed domestic expectations set for women. My mother jokes that I don't own an iron anymore. She thinks this is an insult, but I think my wrinkled clothes are a perfect guage to see that my life is in better balance. When you start to buy that linen dress, calculate the ironing time or the laundry fees, then ask yourself if you'd rather use that time or money to have more fun. Start small, it adds up.

5. Adjust your balance with each new

horse. Like changing horses, each new chapter of your life will require an adjustment in your balance. Some rides are smooth as silk, others seem to jar your bones. But if you stay balanced in the saddle, you can weather the roughest of rides.

6. Life is short, get out and embrace it. There's no better time to get your life in balance than today. You'll find lots of excuses not to do it, because change is tough. Cowgirl Up and start heading down the trail less traveled.

4. Ride the Trail of Adventure

For women who longed for a western adventure in the 1880s, the going was tough. In many areas it was even impossible because societal norms didn't tolerate women even dressing as cowhands. Some cowboy wives and daughters would secretly don their husband's or brother's pants to help rope, doctor and herd the family's cattle and other livestock. The women saw pants as a necessity, not a statement. The men considered pants as cross dressing. Based on the reaction of the cowboys, you'd think these pant-clad women had just shot a man in cold blood. Many cowboys refused to ride with women in pants. Their reputations could be ruined if they were seen cavorting with such wild women of ill repute. So to ride the trail of adventure, women had to first overcome something as simple as being able to dress for the occasion.

To live the same adventures as their male counterparts also meant that cowgirls had to overcome work-related stereotypes as well. Cowboys frequently reminded women that there was no such term as "cowgirl." They believed that work on a ranch was called cowboying for a reason. Cowboys expected women to feed the cattle, stoke the branding fire or ride out with the chuck wagon, but leave the real cowboying to men. A real badge of honor for a woman was to be called a "cowboy-girl." It signaled acceptance. This tradition is still popular today with old hands. While progressive cowboys might call it "ranching," old timers still refer to it as "cowboying."

Cowboy-girls didn't get caught up in semantics. They wanted an adventure of working cattle, riding high in the saddle and sleeping under the stars. It didn't matter what others called them. One cowboy who led the way for cowboy-girls was Willie Mathews.

Willie grew up on the family ranch in Clayton, New Mexico. This cowpoke's father had been a trail boss herding cattle from New Mexico to Montana in the 1800s. Willie's father told grand tales of high adventure on trail rides up the Goodnight-Loving Trail. Willie loved those stories and longed for a taste of this freedom and adventure.

One day in 1884, Willie heard about a trail boss who had come to town looking for some cowboys to drive cattle from New Mexico to Wyoming. For Willie, this was a dream come true. Willie packed some food and clothes, saddled a horse and headed to town to find this trail boss in need of cowboys.

Sam Houston was the hiring trail boss's name—not the legendary Sam Houston of Texas, but an equally famous man who was known for driving some of the largest cattle herds across the Southwest. Sam Houston was a rough but fair man. He was aiming to find some honest, hardworking cowboys for the long cattle drive to Wyoming and this is exactly what he found in Willie. "How much riding experience you got cowboy?" asked Sam. "Been riding and herding on my daddy's ranch all my life," said Willie. "What you think about working in the rain?" asked Sam. "Sun, rain, wind…it don't matter much to me," shrugged Willie. Sam thought Willie was a bit small and too young, but no other men had come for the job. "You're hired!" Sam told the cowboy. "We leave in the morning."

It took a few weeks for Willie's saddle-worn thighs to quit burning from some of the longest rides a cowboy could stand. Some days, Willie thought the sun would never go down. But while the days were long, they were also exhilarating. Willie never knew what the next day would bring—fording rivers, pulling calves out of steep gullies, chasing off coyotes and wolves or admiring the breathtaking scenery. Willie savored the days filled with the sweet smell of prairie sage and the baying of the cattle. When the daylight activities were over, cowboy tales were told by campfire while the night sky lit up with shooting stars. Being new to cowboying, Willie hadn't heard campfire tales and was mesmerized by these seasoned storytellers. Some nights it was ghost stories, other nights amazing tales of cowboy lore or some of the darndest things animals could do. Willie particularly liked the tales of rescuing buffalo calves after mass killings left the babes as orphans. A good cowpoke knew how to get an easy-going heifer to nurse these orphaned buffalo calves. The cowboys lamented that the range had fewer and fewer buffalo.

49

For the next three months, everything went like a dream. Willie's cowboying adventure had come true on one of the most famous cattle trails. Willie had cowboyed with the best and the trail boss seemed to really appreciate the young cowpoke's hard work. Sam Houston thought Willie was about one of the best cowboys he'd ever hired. According to Sam, "That kid would get up on the darkest stormy nights and stay with the cattle until the storm was over. He was good natured, very modest, didn't use any cuss words or tobacco, and was always pleasant…I was so pleased with him that I wished many times that I could find two or three more like him."

Willie loved the adventure, but home and family seemed too far away. Upon reaching the Colorado-Wyoming border, Willie complained to Sam of awful homesick feelings and asked to be paid and excused from the outfit. Sam could see the cowboy was too young to be away from home that long. Sorry to see this reliable cowboy go, Sam paid the cowboy and watched him ride off into the distance.

Later that night, while sitting round the campfire, Sam and his drovers looked up to see someone approaching the camp. To Sam's utter bewilderment, he saw a woman dressed in fine linens and a fancy hat approaching their campsite. Not possible, he thought. As the woman drew closer, she dismounted and approached Sam. "You don't know me, do you Mr. Houston?" the woman said. For several minutes Sam couldn't speak. "Could it be?" he thought. "Kid, is it possible that you're a lady?" Sam asked. Then Willie stuck out her hand and introduced herself as Wilhelmina Mathews. For the first time in four months Sam was at a loss for words. Willie would have given her entire four months pay to have a picture of the look on Sam's face. He was as perplexed as a horse straddling a hitching post.

Sam pulled up a box crate, turned it on end and invited Willie, um Wilhelmina, to join him and the other cowboys by the fire. It was the first time Sam had ever pulled up a seat for a drover who worked for him, and it was the first time any of these drovers had entertained a woman in camp—that is a woman who dressed like a lady. It was a day of firsts for Willie too, for she finally had a campfire tale to tell. "You'd better sit down and explain yourself," said Sam. Willie told them how she had borrowed her brother's clothes and snuck off to Clayton to meet with Sam and hire on as a drover. "What made you dream of doing such a thing?" Sam asked. "I'd always wanted to drive cattle up the Goodnight-Loving Trail," Willie said. "Since women weren't allowed, I became a cowboy." Sam just shook his head in disbelief. Sam had heard of some women wearing pants on their family ranch, but never wearing pants to get a job. Wait until he told the other trail bosses in Wyoming. They weren't going to believe this tale.

Initially, Sam thought the whole Willie episode a comical farce, but then his mind began racing through the past few weeks. He was recalling all the things that had been said in front of this lady on the trail and by the campfire. Willie noticed Sam's face was noticeably red, and she hoped Sam wasn't too angry with her. All the cussing, crotch scratching and farting was coming back to him like a livid nightmare. You'd have thought the whole male sanctum had been breeched based on the squirming around that campfire.

After they all had a good laugh, Willie rose to leave. Stretching out her hand to Sam she said, "I am glad I found you, for I have truly enjoyed myself."

Lessons Learned

Cowgirls of the Wild West enjoyed a good adventure. All of us need a bit of adventure from time to time. We'd be dead if we didn't. But we each define adventure a little differently. For some, a ride with girlfriends to the nearest big city will qualify. For others the definition of adventure is bigger than J.R. Ewing's Dallas ranch, with a dose of dare and dash of thrill.

Willie wanted an adventure and the one she roped was a barn buster. Cross dressing and keeping her sexuality a secret for over three months couldn't have been easy. The cowboys must have suspected something when she didn't pee from the saddle. I wonder how many river baths she had to pass up in order to keep her cover. The stench must have been awful. Yep, she was one driven gal who wanted an adventure and bucked all the norms to get it.

Willie's story should make you think about the last adventure you had. If you can't remember, then it's been too long. You're well overdue! Without a little adventure from time to time, your cowgirl spirit will burn down to a flicker. Life is short, get out and embrace it.

Willie's story should also make you ponder what you'd be willing to sacrifice for the adventure of a lifetime. If you can't sleep in anything but a four-star hotel, your chances for adventure and cowgirl smarts are slim. In fact, I'm not a betting woman, but I'd wager that if you need a lot of pampering you're probably not cowgirl smart. To live a kick-ass life requires some sacrifices, but with a good adventure, you won't even notice.

If your daily routine is void of adventure, here are some ideas for filling your life with a little more adventure.

1. Ride the adventure trail with friends. A trail ride with girlfriends could be just the adventure you need to awaken your cowgirl spirit. If horses aren't your thing, invite friends over and have each bring an unusual foreign dish. Buy some music to match the menu and let the adventure begin.

2. Take a cowgirl adventure trip. Make a pilgrimage to your favorite shrine. I, of course, would recommend the National Cowgirl Museum and Hall of Fame in Fort Worth, Texas, but you may prefer Graceland or New York's Museum of Modern Art.

3. Find your passion. Think about what you're passionate about and enroll in a community college course on that subject. It might be zoology, jewelry making, painting—or better yet, horseback riding.

4. Be daring. Make a lunch date with someone you've always wanted to meet. Take tango lessons. Pitch a tent in your own backyard or a nearby campground and sleep under the stars.

5. Get your cowgirl thrills! Try rock climbing, skydiving or whitewater rafting. Sign up for an adventure travel trip. There are companies that specialize in adventure travel for women and you'll meet others with cowgirl smarts, just like you.

5. Dream as Big as Texas

In the 1800s and early 1900s, when cowgirls started making headlines, women were expected to be demure beings of retirement—certainly not career minded. Thousands and thousands of your female ancestors settled for a life of tea parties, idle gossip and limited activity. They maintained the *status quo* brought to America on boats from the land of English Victorian purity.

Thank God cowgirls didn't settle for the status quo. For them, life had to be charged and roped before it got away. They had dreams as big as Texas. Sure they disobeyed society's rules and therefore weren't invited to boring ladies' teas. But their lives were richer, for they had a keen sense of who they were and what they wanted out of life. It was their bad-girl tendencies which helped them to blaze new paths for the rest of us.

One woman who dreamed big and never settled for the *status quo* was Fanny Seabride from Chicago. Fanny longed to see the West and ride the open plains. Though cowboying was her goal, she knew she would never be hired as a ranch hand, so she traveled to Texas in the 1890s to assume the demure job of governess for a wealthy ranch owner. Fanny figured she could ease into ranch life, help out a bit from atop a horse and slowly be accepted as a full cowhand.

Now the fact that Fanny barely knew her way around a western saddle didn't seem to concern her or dampen her dream at all. But if anyone had asked Fanny upon her arrival in Texas to identify the gelding in the corral, it would have taken some embarrassing underbelly gropes for her to answer intelligently.

At first, Fanny's dream didn't go exactly as planned. To start, the stagecoach journey from Chicago to Texas was a rough one. The passengers bounced from side to side, cramped in the small coach, which was nothing but wood planks atop a wheelbase with no shocks. When the ride wasn't jarring, the heat and cigar smoke was enough to suffocate her. The scenery was breathtaking, but the Indian scares took too much of her breath away. It was no place for a lady, but Fanny wanted to be a cowgirl, so she thought this journey was merely conditioning for what awaited her in Texas.

As it happened, Fanny's employer didn't take kindly to Fanny working from a horse, much less riding astride. Fanny was expected to set a good example for her young charges. Her cowgirl dreams seemed to be fading as fast as the Texas sun on an orange-filled sunset, but her luck would soon change.

One afternoon, Fanny was visiting the famous Horseshoe XX Ranch, when a fence mender was thrown from his horse and injured. The ranch foreman desperately needed someone to ride thirty miles to repair a broken fence line before the cattle spilled out over the open range.

As the men stood scratching their heads, trying to pass the buck on this thankless job, Fanny called out, "I'll mend it!" The cowboys had a good laugh over this. How could a governess in ribbons and curls mend fences? They hadn't finished laughing before Fanny leaped on a mustang armed with a hatchet, wire, staples and a rifle lashed to the saddle. Before they could stop her, Fanny galloped away to repair the damaged fence. You can imagine the look on these cowboys' faces when she returned with the job completed. Though the official account of this story doesn't say, I bet more than one man had to ride out and inspect Fanny's work before believing her.

Having demonstrated her cowboy skills and earned the respect of these ranch hands, she applied for the fence mending job left vacant by the injured cowboy. At first, the owner of the Horseshoe XX Ranch didn't quite know what to make of this governess-gone-wild. He'd never hired a cowboy-girl, but he'd never seen one so skilled and determined. He didn't want to douse her fiery spirit, but he didn't have much faith in women cowboys. Thinking he could dissuade Miss Fanny, the ranch owner tried to frighten her by telling her of the wild animals she would be expected to fight, then he gave her permission to take the job until she was tired. That cowboy had a lot to learn about women.

In 1901, a reporter from *The Denver Times* caught up with Fanny. In four years, she had not only kept the job, but had done remarkably well.

The amazing part of her success is that fence mending really didn't pay well. In fact, it was the lowest job in the cowboy hierarchy—cowboys universally despised and avoided it. Cowboys would rather be knee deep, scooping stalls than riding fences. Being a woman of many talents, Fanny found a way to turn that lowly job into a cash cow. You see, while riding the fences, she became a bounty hunter for neighboring ranchers who were tired of having their livestock poached by local wildlife. Ranchers paid her handsomely to keep their livestock safe.

The Denver Times reported that Fanny killed and scalped 531 coyotes, 49 lobo wolves, 39 wildcats, 13 hyenas and 2 black bears. From her profitable bounty hunter business, Fanny saved enough to purchase 1,000 head of cattle and a sizable ranch of her own. Wouldn't you like to have seen the look on her dates' faces when they saw pelts covering every square inch of her ranch house. It puts a whole new spin on decorating with animal prints.

Fannie knew how to dream big and use her cowgirl smarts. She took the job she could get and turned it into her cowgirl dream. Fanny never wanted to mend fences and kill animals, but it was a necessary step toward achieving her dreams of being a cowgirl. With hard work, her dream to be a cowgirl had become as big and as real as Texas—she was now her own ranch boss.

Another cowgirl who was resourceful in keeping her dream alive was Ms. William Mannix of Montana. She was a child of the frontier, born in 1876. With ranching in her blood, she married William Mannix in 1898 and worked cattle on their ranch between Helmville and Avon, Montana. Ranching was the hard life she knew and loved. But the work only became harder when her husband was stricken with polio, leaving him crippled. With at least eleven mouths to feed, ten being her children, she took over management of the ranch, taking the smaller children along in a horse cart when she had to ride the ranch.

If life wasn't hard enough, one winter her entire family caught the flu, which in those times killed many a frontier family. With snow on the ground, she had worse thoughts than her family in sick beds. She had twenty-seven cows to be milked and hundreds of cattle to be fed. With flu on the ranch, she was lucky to have even one hired helper. Her Christmas gift came in the form of an answered prayer—all of her family survived the flu. But her real problems had only just begun.

Even with her children well enough to work the ranch, Mrs. Mannix still couldn't make ends meet. So she took a job driving the stage twice a week between Finn and Avon, Montana. She drove that stage for fifteen years to keep her ranch afloat. Many ranch wives took jobs outside the ranch to pay expenses, but few of these women were also the ranch manager. It was pure grit, determination and unbelievable stamina that fueled her dream to be a rancher.

When an unrelenting drought drove Ms. Mannix's hay bills to forty dollars a cow, and cattle were selling at twenty dollars a head, she was finally forced to sell her ranch. But she vowed to get her dream ranch back. She spent twenty years working and saving until her vow was fulfilled and she repurchased her ranch. Hers was a dream that she would not let die.

It was reported that when Ms. Mannix was seventy, her sons told her to retire. Being her own ranch boss for half a decade, she didn't take to others givng the orders on her own ranch. The next morning, she saddled up before dawn, rode out on her own and didn't return until long after dinner. Her sons finally saw the futility of their worries and insisted their mom return to ride with the ranch crew. Her sons should have known that a woman like their mother would not go down without a fight.

Ms. Mannix never gave up her dream to own and run her ranch. Not flu, drought, financial ruin or headstrong sons would stand between her and a dream as big as her home state of Montana. It is this kind of tenacity and resourcefulness that makes a woman cowgirl smart, and it's her dreams that motivate her beyond what others think is impossible.

Lessons Learned

What would you be willing to do to attain your dreams? Is taking an entry paying job stopping you from getting started? Are you not saving for a house or college education simply because you don't believe your dream will come true? I think there's a lot to learn from Fanny. She had a dream as big as Texas and the passion to make it come true. And in the process, she helped buck the stereotypes placed on women. She wanted more out of life and she worked her dream until it became her reality.

Ms. Mannix was equally determined to keep her dream alive and overcome all odds to ensure her dreams became reality. No job was too tough and no sum of money to large to deter her drive.

My advice is to go out and pursue your dreams and leave those grandstand jockeys sitting on the bench. Like my daddy used to say: "Don't worry about biting off more than you can chew, your mouth's probably bigger than you think." Here are my suggestions for making your own cowgirl dreams come true:

1. Think outside the ranch! Whether it's your family, your spouse or your community trying to set the rules, don't settle for the *status quo*. Dream big! For example, just because you come from a long line of career nurses, or most of the women in your town don't go to college, doesn't mean you have to be a sheep and follow suit. Listen to your heart, blaze a path of your own choosing and rely on your inner strength to rope your dreams.

2. If you find yourself in a hole, the first

thing you should do is stop digging. Cowgirls don't whine and demand pitty for their problems—they cowgirl up. Access your situation, then set goals to reach your dreams. Think like a cowgirl and be determined to become whoever you want to be.

3. If you can't start in the job you want, take the job you can get. Be tenacious and relentless until you earn the position you desire. After all, there's no place around the cowgirl campfire for a quitter's bedroll. Lots of women have started at the bottom and worked their way to the top. You can too!

4. Let your dreams be known. Don't be shy about stating your intentions and demanding to be considered for any type of appointment in your association or organization. If you don't make your dreams known, how can others help you make them a reality?

6. Be Tough, But Be Feminine

When I entered the business world, I found I was frequently the only woman around the conference table. I like working with men, so this never really bothered me. I was generally treated with respect and my ideas were given consideration. But I noticed that senior management didn't think it necessary to groom me for promotion simply because I was a woman. In their minds, women didn't really want to be in charge. Besides, they figured I'd be having babies soon and would resign.

In order to be taken more seriously as a candidate for promotion, I tried to be more like the guys. My logic was that since I was running with the boys, I should dress like the boys. So I bucked the corporate dress code that stipulated women were to wear skirts and I started wearing pantsuits. When in Rome, do as the Romans, right? I couldn't have been more wrong. After a few days in pants, my boss asked me if I was "growing balls"—not that he had any. A male co-worker in my department told me that he liked me better in skirts so he could look at my legs. I told him I liked him better in hats so I didn't have to look at his bald head—that went over as well as you'd imagine. My pants-wearing strategy failed. I realized that I had to be tough and feminine to be taken seriously. These men didn't want me to dress like a man, they wanted me to act like one.

In my eagerness to work a man's job, but still remain feminine, I asked myself, "How did cowgirl compete in early rodeos?" They were competing in a man's sport, why didn't they dress like men?

In my search for cowgirl smarts, I learned that thinking and acting like a cowgirl doesn't mean giving up your femininity. Cowgirls knew that you could be tough and still wear skirts. In fact, giving up femininity went against much of what these first rodeo cowgirls believed in. I'm sure many cowgirls were quick to ditch their corsets behind the first rock outside of town, but it wasn't a feminist, bra-burning statement. It was purely for comfort. Had sports bras been invented, I bet these cowgirls would've gladly embraced them. (Nike® could have made a fortune.)

I found that cowgirls experienced a similar but more severe reaction than I did when I tested out my new pants. In the 1800s, a woman riding astride in pants caused quite a commotion. Some cowhands wouldn't have been seen riding with a woman in pants. It wasn't uncommon for women in pants to be thrown out of town or even put in jail, because back then, many towns prohibited women in pants or even riding astride.

It didn't seem to matter that dresses combined with ranch work spelled danger. On more than one occasion, a woman's skirt got caught in the stirrup, and she was dragged beneath her horse. Trick riders found skirts even more hazardous as they vaulted from one side of their horse to the other. Just think about it. These first women ranchers were out on an isolated ranch roping and branding cattle, why didn't they just wear pants? Many didn't because they reveled in their femininity which in Victorian times meant always wearing a dress. You might think them crazy, but their femininity was important to them.

Probably the most famous skirt-clad cowgirl was Lucille Mulhall, who at the age of twenty was deemed the greatest horsewoman in America. Lucille was born in 1885, and was raised on a ranch in Oklahoma. Her father, an excellent horseman, made her an exemplary rider and roper at a very early age. When she was eight, she asked her father for her own herd of cattle. Jokingly, her father told her she could have all the cattle she could brand. That afternoon, Lucille's father found she had roped and branded twenty calves, using the buckle on her cinch as a branding iron. Instead of punishing Lucille for ruining a perfectly good cinch, he helped Lucille register her own cattle brand of "LM" and assisted her in rebranding her newly acquired cattle with an appropriate branding iron.

While her father beamed with pride over Lucille's amazing skills with a rope, her mother was less than thrilled. She saw her little girl being reared as a boy. Her solution was to send Lucille to a convent for training in the gentler arts. While Lucille excelled at her studies, the nuns couldn't tame this daring cowgirl. When the nuns gave up on Lucille, she returned to the ranch and honed her roping skills. At ten years of age, Lucille was roping cattle with better success than many of her father's ranch hands. (Don't you know that went over well?)

In 1898, Colonel Theodore Roosevelt attended one of her father's shows. He was amazed at Lucille's roping skills. At thirteen years of age, she was riding and roping in her father's show—the Congress of Rough Riders and Ropers. Roosevelt was so impressed with the girl that he invited her to dinner. Lucille in turn invited him to her ranch. Three days later, Roosevelt arrived at the ranch and watched Lucille rope and ride a wild horse. He jokingly dared her to rope a wolf, promising that if she succeeded, she could be his guest at the inaugural dinner when he was sworn in as vice president. To his amazement, she returned only three hours later dragging a huge dead wolf. "How did you kill it?" asked Roosevelt. She explained that she simply roped it and then killed it with her stirrup iron. There was no doubt about it, this girl was TOUGH!

Tradition has it that Lucille was the first female to ever be called "cowgirl." Prior to Lucille earning the title of "cowgirl" after her performance at the St. Louis fair in 1899, women were called "cowboy-girls." A year later, when Lucille was only fourteen years old, her notoriety as "the first cowgirl" spread nationwide when the press covered this petite girl and her daring skill at stopping a bull from trampling a fellow competitor to death. As it was reported, a supposed senorita (her gender was debated by many) was attempting to ride a bull in an exposition. When the senorita was thrown, the announcer dispatched their best roper, Lucille, to get the bull away from the woman. Instead of roping the bull, Lucille jumped on the bull's back and rode him until her brother relieved her. She was assisting in the way she thought best. Again, that girl was tough.

At fifteen, Lucille performed in Des Moines, Iowa, where she roped five horses simultaneously. This may seem amazing to you, but Lucille was probably disappointed because she was capable of roping eight. Not bad for a young teenager who only stood five feet tall. Lucille went on to win steer roping contests across the West. But it was her performance in Wichita Kansas in 1904 that caused her popularity to soar to mythic proportion. When her steer was set loose in the arena, it jumped a five-foot-tall fence and ran for freedom. Not to be deterred, Lucille and her trusty horse Governor leaped the fence and roped the steer outside the arena. Her time was not only competitive, it won her first place in the steer roping event.

I could go on and on recalling the feats of this remarkable cowgirl, but I'll stop here to tell you the most amazing part of Lucille's accomplishments. Lucille did it all in a skirt! She always wore a floor length split skirt with a fresh white silk shirtwaist and her hair in curls tied with a bow at the back of her neck. It seems her training in the convent and her mother's insistence on lady-like behavior must have taken hold. She was roping and tying steers from the ground in as little as forty seconds—in a long skirt! Despite working in a man's world and beating men at their own games, Lucille paraded her femininity in the arena and on the silver screen always wearing a skirt.

Even when cowgirl performers began wearing bloomers around 1912, and later jodhpurs in the early 1920s, Lucille held firm to what she considered more feminine attire. She wanted to make the point that tough girls can wear skirts too.

Lessons Learned

Even though Lucille once took a serious fall when her skirt got caught in her stirrup as she flew from the saddle to tie her roped steer, she refused to ever give up her skirts. You may not agree with Lucille subjecting herself to the danger of wearing skirts in rodeos, but you have to admire Lucille, because she reveled in her femininity. She had her own definition of femininity and she wasn't changing her standards to suit anyone else.

Lucille wasn't confined by the rules of society. She chose not to accept the growing trend toward what she considered more masculine dress. She competed on her own terms. Lucille will always be remembered not only as the first cowgirl, but as a skilled, tough woman who never traded her femininity for a rope and a steer.

I value Lucille's story because at a time when I was learning to run with the big boys, she made me realize that I didn't have to trade in my love of fashion for a seat in the men's club. Whether I wore pants or a skirt, I could be the woman I loved being. I learned that my work eventually spoke louder than my gender or my clothes. Here are some ideas on femininity that I'm sure Lucille would approve of:

1. Don't trade your femininity for a man's world. Sure there are still bastions of sexist males in this world who might initially think less of you when you're all dolled up. But Lucille and the rest of your cowgirl sisters are counting on you to change these beliefs one man at a time.

2. Motherhood shouldn't change your feminine mystique. Sure chasing kids is easier done in overalls and wash-n-wear duds. But set aside one night a week when you can step into something sexy and feel like a lady.

3. Don't scoff at chivalry. Women unaccustomed to southern gentlemen might find it odd when men won't enter an elevator before women. I've even witnessed a female executive curse a waiter for asking, "What can I get you ladies to drink." Ease up! Is being a lady really all that bad? Chivalry is not an affront to your level of intelligence it's a show of respect. Learn to revel in this admiration of your femininity.

4. Show others that feminine is hip. I once read about two women who bought an auto repair shop and painted the whole building pink. They hired mostly women mechanics and furnished them with floral overalls. Women customers were treated with an unusual degree of respect. It was pure marketing genius for attracting female customers—and big surprise—men came in droves. Don't be afraid to show how much you enjoy being a woman.

5. Pink boots won't make you a lady. If you think pink boots or lace shirts instantly make you more feminine, you're wrong. Being feminine is not just your dress, but how you feel about and portray the woman inside. If you learn to love the feminine side of yourself, it will show through to others. You'll appear feminine even in the dirtiest of coveralls.

7. Attack Life Like It's a 1000 Pound Steer

By the turn of the twentieth century, many cowgirls had been breaking horses on the family ranch and riding bulls at local rodeos for several years. The tide was turning and women became anxious to compete in the men's rodeo events. Cowgirls could compete in trick riding and relay races, but they longed to strut their stuff in the more daring events. Women were first allowed to enter calf and steer roping, and by 1913 a handful of cowgirls were frequently challenging men at bronc and bull riding. Nevertheless, only a couple fearless cowgirls dared to enter bulldogging contests.

"Bulldogging" is what we now call steer wrestling. In this event, the horse and rider stand behind a line and don't begin their chase until the steer has a head start. The steer wrestler is assisted by a hazer, a cowboy riding horseback on the opposite side of the steer who is tasked with keeping the steer running in a straight line. When the bulldogger's horse pulls up even with the steer, the bulldogger drops down the side of her horse and grabs the bull by the horns. She digs her heels into the dirt and uses her leverage on the horns to tip the steer over. The timer stops the clock when the bull is on its side with all four legs pointing the same direction. Today, steer wrestling is called "the big man's event" and with good reason; at the National Rodeo Finals in Las Vegas in 1997, the average steer wrestler weighed 215 pounds.

In 1913, Tillie Baldwin was the first cowgirl to attempt bulldogging, but she never entered the contest again. It wasn't until 1924, at the Fort Worth Rodeo, that Fox Hastings became known as the first cowgirl to routinely appear as a bulldogger. Several years later, when cowgirls like Claire Belcher, Vivian White, Grace Runyan and Lucille Richards got up the courage to wrestle steers, rodeo producers began adding ladies' bulldogging as a competitive event. But it didn't last long and neither did the ladies. Bulldogging is intrinsically dangerous and many discontinued the event due to injuries.

What would it take for you to think you could wrestle a steer to the ground? I'm guessing most women would never consider it. For those who do, it takes a LOT of courage, a little craziness and a well-thought-out plan. Not surprisingly, Fox didn't jump from her horse and turn a steer on her first try. She realized it would take a calculated plan and years of preparation to succeed. Nothing great ever comes easy, and cowgirls don't expect it to.

Fox started with strength training. Then for months she practiced the two critical skills a bulldogger needs: speed off the horse and a body position that leverages the weight of the bull. When she moved to live steers, she started small and worked up to larger animals. In the eighteen months leading up to her first performance, she broke her leg three times. Now you might think she was crazy for trying this dangerous sport, but she wasn't crazy in how she went about preparing for it. She attacked her first 1,000-pound steer using a calculated and practiced plan of attack. Cowgirls know that with any goal of this size, you need a plan and focused determination. By using your cowgirl smarts, you can do anything, including wrestling a 1000 pound steer to the ground.

Fox went on to perform at dozens of rodeos and Wild West shows. Her record-breaking bulldogging time of seventeen seconds was tough for most men to beat. Not only was she proficient at bulldogging, she was a charismatic performer. Dozens of published pictures of Fox show her smiling from the dirt floor of the arena, with the horns of a 1,000 pound steer wrapped around her waist. She became one of the most interviewed and photographed cowgirls of the late 1920s. She used her cowgirl smarts not only to master steer wrestling, but to make her success known. In this way, her long months of training became even more profitable.

Isora DeRacy Young is a Cowgirl Hall of Fame Honoree like Fox. Isora started roping and tying cattle at a relatively late age compared to other cowgirls. In 1924 at the age of nineteen she moved to Pecos, Texas, and joined a roping club. She practiced weekly and grew to love the sport claiming she would "rope anything, anytime, anywhere they'd let me." Isora recalls that most of the time she roped for a set fee per calf. With the high cost of traveling around the country to compete, she made sure that she missed very few calves.

At a rodeo in Salinas, California, the announcer called out, "Here is the gal from Texas who can rope and tie a 300-pound calf in less time than I can wrap a pound of hamburger." Isora remembers the man made her feel "ten feet tall." But she knew it was a lot of hard work and planning that got her to that moment. To hone her roping and tying skills, Isora purchased a small calf. She roped that calf twice a day until it weighed 400 pounds. By starting small and working up to a large calf, she was able to rope, flip and tie any calf on the rodeo circuit in record time. She stayed focused on her goal and used a calculated plan of advancement to achieve her goal. She truly used her cowgirl smarts.

Lessons Learned

Attacking life like it's 1,000-pound steer, doesn't mean you must gather your courage and come nose to nose with a calf or even a steer. It means that no goal is too big if you approach it with careful planning and a focused determination. Most cowgirls never believe they can wrestle a steer, or become a CEO or be elected to the United States Senate—but they can if they attack the task with a strategic course of action. A woman with cowgirl smarts can accomplish anything if she starts small and follows a calculated plan for reaching the top. Below are other cowgirl characteristics of highly successful cowgirls:

1. Always have a trail map. No matter what your goal, you need to develop a plan and have trail map for getting there. Once your map or guide is in place, give it everything you have. Be reasonable. Start small and work up to it.

2. Don't ask, "Can I?" ask, "How can I?" Don't waste energy worrying if you're able to close the distance between where you are now and where you want to be. Focus your energy on finding a trail that will close the gap with as little effort as possible. If you doubt yourself, your horse and others will too

3. When the going gets tough, focus on your reward. Whatever your goal, you must know why you want to achieve it—the why is the reward. Your motive could be fame, happiness or simply self-satisfaction, but every goal has a reward. You'll need to want that reward badly enough to stay the course of your training. Horses like working for carrots, and you will too.

4. Believe you can rope a miracle. Be a believer in small miracles; they happen every day. Lots of women beat enormous odds to reach their goals—not because they're lucky, but because they work hard and they believe in themselves.

5. Make your goal to have fun. Sometimes focusing too much on winning debilitates us. As a young swimmer, I always swam faster in workouts than I did at meets. I let the pressure of winning overwhelm me. When I decided to just have fun, I swam faster and enjoyed it more. Ensure that your goal includes having fun.

8. Always Saddle Your Own Horse

The National Cowgirl Hall of Fame in Fort Worth, Texas, uses cowgirl Connie Reeves' motto as its own: "Always Saddle Your Own Horse." As any cowgirl knows, you should always saddle your own horse to ensure the horse is sound and the saddle is safe. But the motto has deeper meaning when you live life by Connie Reeves' rules. She suggested you always saddle your own horse because cowgirls should "do for themselves" and "pull their share of the work load."

It's a point of honor with cowgirls that they are strong enough to hoist the saddle and use their own judgment to see that the cinch is correctly positioned for the horse and adequately tightened to ensure a safe ride. It takes strength to lift a forty pound saddle as high as your head, particularly for shorter cowgirls. Even tightening the cinch on a good-sized horse can be difficult for shorter cowgirls, but cowgirls wouldn't dream of asking for help. These are the rules of the ranch and the rules cowgirls ride by.

To have someone else saddle her horse would make a self-respecting cowgirl ashamed, because it implies she isn't capable. A real cowgirl would never stand for that. Connie Douglas Reeves taught thousands of Texas girls not only to ride, but to approach life like they would their horse. She taught them not to expect others to do their work for them, to be independent, to be self-reliant and to be responsible. It was Connie's cowgirl creed and it was how she instilled cowgirl smarts into the minds of thousands of young Texas girls.

Many extraordinary cowgirls think of themselves as simple cowgirls. Such was the case with Connie—a true cowgirl who led an extraordinary life helping others from atop a horse. Despite her long list of achievements and awards, humble is how most people describe her. When inducted into the National Cowgirl Hall of Fame, Connie commented, "I just don't know what all this fuss is about." Connie died in 2003 at the age of 101, after being thrown from her horse. Millions read the story of her life in newspapers across the United States and longed to live and die as Connie had, doing what she loved.

Connie's vivacious personality and showmanship came from her mother while her keen intellect came from her father, who was a district judge in Eagle Pass, Texas. Following in her father's footsteps, Connie was one of the first female graduates from the University of Texas Law School. Had the Depression not sidelined the launch of her legal career in 1925, Connie would have been one of the first female lawyers in the nation. While the Depression may have ended her legal career, it opened the door to a life of horses and teaching.

Upon leaving The University of Texas at

Austin, Connie took a teaching position in San Antonio to support her parents. But being an ordinary teacher wasn't in the cards for Connie. As an English and speech teacher at Jefferson High School in 1932, she formed Texas' first pep squad named The Lassos that still exists today. The Lassos consisted of 150 students performing synchronized lasso routines and a smaller group that performed rope tricks on horseback. Connie's squad was featured at the 1939 World's Fair, was the subject of a Hollywood movie and performed for President Roosevelt. Connie's creed proved to be an important ingredient for training teenage girls, but it also developed a deep sense of cowgirl smarts that remained with these girls through their adult life.

During her summer breaks from teaching high school, Connie taught riding at Camp Waldemar for girls in Hunt, Texas. Since 1926, Camp Waldemar has taken pride in building character in young girls, and they couldn't have found a better role model than Connie. Connie's summer job at Camp Waldemar soon became her lifelong passion that lasted sixty-seven years and spanned three generations of Texas' daughters. Carter Tatum, a third generation Waldemar camper feels the most important thing Connie taught her had nothing to do with horses. "She taught us to never stop going, physically or mentally, and to not let time or people get in the way of that momentum." By teaching riding into her 90's, Connie was a great role model for all of us. Though she only stood five-feet-two-inches tall, campers remember her as somewhat intimidating and very powerful. "When Connie gave you a compliment," said Tatum, "you knew you had done really well. All of us wanted to do our best for Connie—we had so much respect for her."

But respect for this cowgirl didn't stop with the over 30,000 girls she taught at Camp Waldemar. In 1997, Connie was inducted into the National Cowgirl Hall of Fame in Fort Worth and in 1998 she became the only female recipient of the National Cowboy Hall of Fame's Chester A. Reynolds Award for outstanding achievement. At her award ceremony, a standing ovation was led by a room of western icons such as Tom Selleck and Larry Gatlin. The Texas Chamber of Commerce honored Connie as one of Texas' 100 Most Outstanding Women and the Freedom Forum gave her the Free Spirit Award, previously bestowed upon Barbara Bush and Chuck Yeager.

Connie's forty-three-year marriage to Jack Reeves was as remarkable as her equestrienne career, in that it represented a true partnership. Jack was a professional rodeo cowboy who retired to work their ranch in Junction, Texas. Their partnership started and ended with caring for the animals they loved. After Jack died in 1985, Connie wrote about him in her book, *I Married A Cowboy*. The book revealed a well-kept secret: Connie wrote as beautifully as she rode.

Connie's tenacity for life was unmatched.

On a trail ride at age ninety-two, Connie was thrown from her horse while trying to assist a rider whose horse was also spooked by a hornets' nest on the ground. In the process, Connie fell on the hornets' nest and sustained broken ribs, a collapsed lung, a broken wrist and too many stings to count. Only a month later, Connie went to Arizona for a trail ride and bragged to friends that she was the oldest employee in Texas to file for workman's compensation. Never one to miss a good ride, Connie saddled her own horse at the age of 100 and rode in the parade that celebrated the opening of the new Cowgirl Hall of Fame building.

Her life was cut short at 101 years when her favorite horse, Dr. Pepper, stumbled, and tossed her to the ground. In the emergency room, the attending doctor demanded to know who let this 101-year-old woman go riding? What a dope! He obviously didn't know Connie Reeves or the will of a cowgirl. Given the tough old gal she was, it wasn't the fall that killed her. She died of cardiac arrest several days later. "In the hospital, Connie told me she had a dream that her horse told her it was time to retire," said Marsha Elmore, who was Connie's former boss at Camp Waldemar. "In a month, Connie would have been 102 and she was still planning and writing speeches for upcoming events." Texas lost one of its western treasures that day. Connie was a legendary woman with the strength and character as big as the state in which she lived.

Hundreds of equestriennes attribute their horse sense and riding skills to Connie, but for many women the most valuable lesson Connie taught them was to "always saddle your own horse—don't expect others to do it for you." It was Connie's way of teaching girls to always carry their own load. Thanks to the National Cowgirl Hall of Fame, Connie's cowgirl smarts will be passed to girls for generations to come.

Lessons Learned

"Always saddle your own horse" is a great cowgirl smarts lesson to teach your kids—goodness knows teaching kids responsibility is important. But as a mature woman, the lesson still has great value in that you shouldn't expect others to take care of you. Too often I see perfectly capable women complaining that this person or that service company hasn't come to help them—when in fact they aren't helpless. They only believe they are helpless. And when they stand and complain that someone isn't coming to their rescue, well, my cowgirl heart doesn't bleed for them. I just feel sorry for them.

Independence is a pivotal point in becoming cowgirl smart. Cowgirls don't expect others to take care of them. Their independence is a point of honor and it makes their lives more fulfilled to know they can make it on their own. This doesn't mean she won't be appreciative to a husband or friend who unclogs her sink or carries her saddle to the tack room. But the key is that she knows she can do it herself and that help from others is a gift, not an expectation or a necessity.

There's one last lesson that I'm sure all of Connie's cowgirls at Camp Waldemar experienced, and I hope you will too. It is the added joy and satisfaction felt when you know your accomplishments are 100% your own. Success is so much sweeter when you know you did it yourself.

Here are some ideas to keep you saddling your own horse:

1. Stand on your own two feet. Never expect others to do for you. Take pride in doing for yourself. It will make you a more independent and confident cowgirl that others will want to be around.

2. Pull your own load. Be sure that others can always count on you to do your share of the work. At the end of the trail, there's always room by the campfire for a cowgirl who's pulled her share of the work. The same is true for playtime: cowgirls who attend every party, but never give one themselves, will find the campfire extinguished when they come to visit.

3. To ensure it's done right, do it yourself. I've tried all my life to learn to delegate, but sometimes the best way to ensure a job well done, is to do it yourself. Learn when to accept other cowgirls' work as good enough, and when your cowgirl smarts are needed to do the job right.

4. Don't blame others. If your cinch is loose and your saddle turns, you have no one to blame but yourself. When a task is critical enough that it affects you, your children or your livelihood, never let others complete it for you—particularly if you intend to complain about the outcome.

5. There's more than one way to saddle a horse. If you're busy saddling your own horse, you shouldn't have time to critique others. Remember that there's usually more than one way to get a job done and your way is not the only way.

9. Rein in Your Fears

While it's fun to remember the adventurous aspects of the Wild West, women also lived through its inherent dangers. In the 1800s, there were outlaws with guns, wagon trains surrounded by Indians, unrelenting weather beating down make-shift cabins, stampeding cattle, isolation from neighbors and weeks of riding into the unknown.

There's no doubt about it. Hollywood may have glamorized the Old West, but the truth be told, it was dangerous. Cowgirls had scads of reasons to be fearful on many different levels. But an important characteristic that differentiated the successful cowgirl from the not so successful cowgirl was an ability to rein in her fears and overcome self-doubt.

Life on a ranch was a lonely existence for women who stayed home to break horses and watch children while their husbands rode herd. Many women, left alone for weeks and months at a time, would become hysterical from fear and have to be shipped back to the comforts of the city. Overcoming fear and self-doubt was fundamental to successfully ranching the West. Women learned to survive by their wits. Those who questioned their abilities to take on strange new tasks in an unfamiliar land were paralyzed by their own self-doubt.

Cowgirls faced the same two types of fears

that we do today: emotional and physical. Just like you, they asked themselves, "Can I survive it?" and "Can I do it?" Just like you, cowgirls had to look both types of fears in the face and laugh; otherwise, they wouldn't have made it. The fact that so many gathered their skirts and climbed on the backs of unbroken horses doesn't seem so amazing in light of the day-to-day fear of survival they had already lived through.

The autobiography of Elizabeth Smith Collins, a Montana rancher during the 1880s and 1890s, reads like a dime-store western. As a woman, she had a tougher time than most men living through Indian attacks, filthy mining towns and an all-male cattle business. She was forced to face her fears over and over again.

Traveling between Illinois and Mexico more than a dozen times with her father, Elizabeth—as a young girl—honed the skill of standing down her fear. The trip involved a wagon trail that few pioneers ever wanted to travel even once in their lives. On one of these trips she was taken and held captive by Sioux Indians until her brother led a military party to find and free her.

According to Elizabeth, she was so terrified at what the Sioux might do to her that she attempted to kill herself by swallowing the poisonous match tips she had in her pocket. When she coughed up the wet match tips, the phosphorous gave off a glow in the dark, leading her Indian guard to believe she had magical powers. Gathering her wits, she rubbed the phosphorous on her cheeks to give the appearance of her having even greater magical powers. With this trickery, she managed to stay unharmed and even revered by the tribe. Now I wouldn't call her attempted suicide fearless, but her ability to use her newfound "magic" to bravely face the Indians was certainly admirable.

Elizabeth's younger years prepared her for the many obstacles she faced trying to settle in Montana before the turn of the century. She married Nat Collins in 1874, but when he was injured in a mining accident, they decided to go into ranching. It is unclear who decided to start the ranch, but it soon became evident—despite the fact that Nat was unable to ride—that it was the right occupation for Elizabeth. Normally, she sold her cattle to passing cattle drivers, but she was forced to accept only a fraction of what the cattle were worth in Chicago. Finally overcoming her fear of taking her own cattle to Chicago, she hired some drovers and herded her cattle to the train depot.

Elizabeth successfully pushed her cattle for weeks to reach the train depot, but upon arrival, the railroad refused to let her ride in the caboose with the other ranchmen because it was against the rules. For ten days she telegraphed to all the depots down the line, until finally the cowboys threatened to boycott the railroad if she wasn't allowed on the train. How they would have carried out their boycott is a mystery to me, since there wasn't exactly an alternative rail line. It's more likely they threatened to herd their cattle onto the tracks. Through the aid of her competitors, she was finally allowed to board the train—where the cattlemen gave her a round of cheers and the title of Cattle Queen of Montana. In her day, Elizabeth's bravery was sometimes taken as foolery, but there's no doubt that she never let self-doubt creep under her hat.

Alice Greenough of Red Lodge, Montana, was often called "crazy," but never a "fool." Like Elizabeth, Alice was fearless, but she lived for rodeo rather than ranching. Rodeo was Alice's passion and she appeared completely fearless when it came to bronc busting, steer riding or traveling the world unescorted. If you look up "fearless" in the cowgirl dictionary, I'd swear Alice's name would be there. She was a tough rodeo gal and won her fair share of rodeos in the 1920s and 1930s, even traveling to Australia and the Far East by herself for exhibitions and contests. But the ride that probably tested her fear factor the most took place in Spain.

In 1932, Alice signed a contract to ride steers at the bullfights in Spain. But when she arrived in Madrid, she found they intended for her to ride their toughest fighting bulls, not roping steers. Alice could have gotten out of her contract by pleading mistaken bovine identity, but she wasn't one to let her fear get the best of her. To the amazement of the Spaniards, she rode bull after bull until they let her out of her contract—not because she couldn't ride the bulls, but because the men's pride couldn't take her success. You can imagine that if matadors were the bravest of all Spaniards, this petite young cowgirl wasn't helping their image or their machismo.

Alice dominated women's bronc riding in the 1930s, only quitting when the women's event was no longer carried by rodeos. When her competitive days were done, she married and started her own rodeo business from nothing, forging a new life out of raw determination. Alice had a fearless approach to everything she undertook.

In researching Alice's life, I discovered an article she had written in 1937 in a magazine called *Physical Culture: The Personal Problem Magazine*. Amusingly enough, Alice's sage advice about the importance of keeping your mind and body strong, being confident and finding your inner beauty was flanked by sensational advertising for waist reducers—so women could forego exercising—and miracle face creams to build self-confidence. I wonder if women in the 1930s found it as ironic and amusing as I did.

Alice's 1937 article was titled, "What a Cowgirl Wants From Life." In it she made an excellent argument for why cowgirls who exercised their minds as well as their bodies could face any challenge that life threw their way. She contended that learning to ride—especially broncs—trained both your muscles and your mind in a keen sense of self-control. She unabashedly attributed city slickers' widespread unhappiness and need for psychoanalysis to their weakness of mind and body. "You'd never see hysterical, dull-eyed women in the saddle," she wrote.

In her article, Alice contradicted what most believed to be true—that Alice was born fearless. The truth is that she faced a terrible fear each time she straddled a bull—that's why she did it. She became a world champion cowgirl and learned to rope more out of life by overcoming self-doubt and fear.

Lessons Learned

If Alice were writing an advice column today, it would probably be titled, "You Gotta Learn to Stick." In cowgirl lingo, that means you have to learn to overcome your fear and relax if you're going to stay in the saddle. It's not enough to be a great rider; you must be able to control your mind over matter. It's sage advice for both rodeo competitors and city slickers alike.

Relating your twenty-first-century fears to these cowgirls' lives isn't that difficult. If you've ever been the new kid in school, been alone in a new town, taken a job for which you were untrained, paddled a raging rapid or been left by a husband, you can relate to overcoming fear and self-doubt: you were either paralyzed by your fear, or you cowgirled up and moved forward. As in bronc riding contests, you always have two choices when facing your fears: you can pull leather (grab the saddle horn) and be disqualified or you can learn to stick.

I find that most women—especially teens—are smarter and more clever than they think. Most women don't give themselves credit for half of what they're capable. Cowgirls, on the other hand, believe they can do anything. Self-doubt will cripple your confidence faster than your circumstances. So throw a loop around your courage and start living a bigger life!

1. Never let self-doubt creep under your hat. Our own minds can often be the biggest challenge we face. Years ago, a cowboy told me that I was the most insecure, confident person he had ever met. Are you as confident on the inside as you appear on the outside? I was guilty and I've worked ever since to not let self-doubt creep under my hat. I hope you will, too.

2. Don't fold up the chuck wagon at the first sign of trouble. The bigger problems in your life will make you want to ride away at the first sign of trouble. But you have to learn to face fear like a cowgirl and tighten your grip. After you gather your courage and ride it through, you'll have the confidence to mount even meaner bulls.

3. Remember, the seat of your pants is smarter than you think. Cowgirls think dudettes underestimate the power of their common sense—that's because cowgirls have so much of it. Take the lead from cowgirls by believing you can resolve most of your problems with what's already under your hat. 4. Have the courage to follow your heart. Overcoming self-doubt isn't limited to facing problems. It's also about having the courage to follow your passion, to love fully and to show your love to others. Despite all the love-'em and leave-'em country lyrics, cowgirls follow their heart, love big and keep the romance alive.

5. Never stop believing in yourself. At times, people around you will stop believing in you. It happens to every cowgirl sooner or later. Don't let others' judgments come true by internalizing them. Reject their opinion and prove them wrong. Become the person you know you can be.

6. Rise above expectations. Maybe you weren't the lead in your school play or captain of the debate team, but that doesn't mean you won't be best at something one day. When you find a subject or cause that you're passionate about, take it on full throttle. Show others that you've got more between your pigtails than they ever dreamed.

7. Never lose your faith. Faith in yourself and faith in God will help you through the toughest fears you face. Never underestimate faith and never lose it.

10. Dress for Success—the Cowgirl Way!

"Dress for Success" —the phrase brings to mind those 1980s navy suits with red string ties at the neck. Yuck! For women with cowgirl smarts, the phrase means dressing to make a statement or simply indulging the wild-child busting to get out. Now, I'm not suggesting you recreate a J-Lo fashion moment and let your boobs hang out in front of millions of TV viewers—unless of course you actually look like Jennifer Lopez. What I AM suggesting is that you take a lesson from a few Wild West cowgirls who really knew how to dress for success.

A great example is Prairie Rose Henderson—a cowgirl who really knew how to dress for success. No boring attire for her. She was as much about showmanship as she was about cowgirl skill, but she found that performing trick riding in a skirt was not only difficult, it was dangerous. Imagine vaulting off your horse, from side to side, in a floor length split skirt? Having a whole lot more cowgirl smarts than modesty, Rose modified her split riding skirt (what we call culottes) into a new style of western bloomers by removing the button-over flap on the front of her skirt and tying the bottom of each culotte leg at the knee. These bloomers were scandalous in Victorian times—akin to rodeoing in a bikini today.

Until Rose made bloomers a fashion state-ment, stodgy Victorian types would rather see cowgirls risk being dragged by their skirts than show their legs in bloomers. Go figure? And don't even let me get started on the dangers of rodeo-ing in a boned corset. You'd have to be nuts!

Many historic accounts claim Tillie Bald-win was the first cowgirl to wear bloomers in 1913 at a Winnipeg rodeo; however, there are pictures of Rose Henderson in bloomers in 1910. What Tillie wore was a conservative Norwegian gymnastic uniform with bloused legs. What Rose wore were flamboyant bloomers that soon became her wild-woman trademark. Why not pants you ask? In the privacy of your own ranch pasture, a cowgirl might wear her brother or husband's pants, but performing cowgirls were seen by many as "sexual deviants" for wanting to play at a man's game. So to play it conservative, cowgirls in rodeo and Wild West shows didn't risk wearing pants until 1924. That was the year Vera McGinnis wowed audiences at the Fort Worth Rodeo with her Spanish costume of white bell-bottomed pants. Prior to Vera's risqué pants outing, the closest cowgirls came to pants were bloused jodhpurs which were actually bloomers with buttons down the calf.

Riding in bloomers sure brought Rose the attention she wanted, but it faded as other women followed suit. So Rose cranked it up a notch. She began performing her trick riding in brightly colored satin bloomers and feather-trimmed jackets that she made herself—not that she could have found these outfits in any Sears & Roebuck catalog. By today's standards, Rose's outfits looked more like a Victorian gymnast working the red light district than a world famous equestrienne. By Victorian standards her dress was sensational. As if the costumes weren't enough, she ended her rides with a grand kick-stepping sweep around the arena while waving her arms high in the air like a rodeo queen gone wild. She greeted the roaring crowd like old friends.

To say Rose was flamboyant was an understatement. To say she was smart as a cowgirl was dead right. Everywhere she went, she was recognized for her outrageous, but feminine, style. Rodeoing in satin and feathers paid off for Rose. She had successfully used her cowgirl smarts and wild-girl style to draw attention to her world-class riding. This recognition earned her better paying jobs in Wild West shows and rodeos across the US and in Europe. But just as important, it satisfied Rose's own creative style.

Rose's wild-woman dress paid off for other cowgirls as well. Her riding and costume changes created such a sensation that many rodeos began including more women riders in their programs. But none could match Rose's outrageous personal style, infectious laugh, and real horsemanship. For years, she was one of the highest paid and frequently photographed cowgirls in the world. She was the J-Lo of the rodeo!

Lessons Learned

There are several reasons you should follow this cowgirl's lead. First, its effective, but more importantly, it's fun. For example, I have friends in sales that use signature styles to make them more memorable to customers. When all women were wearing blue suits, they wore red. When women started wearing red power suits, they wore all black. The lesson Rose taught me was to use my wardrobe carefully to further my career and to indulge my creative spirit.

While this story recommends making yourself more memorable, other situations may be better won by blending in. There's a right and wrong venue for wild-child outfits, so use your cowgirl smarts to know one from the other. The point is, whether you need outrageous dress or work clothes for construction, either can be accomplished with your own creative style and feminine touch.

I've identified one drawback to this dress-for-success plan: sometimes, when you're enjoying a good dress-for-success moment, some folks just won't approve. Much like Prairie Rose I sometimes find a few people who don't appreciate my fashion sense, but I push on, proving that while my attire may draw attention to my work, it doesn't effect my ability to get the job done. Women who scorn your wardrobe more than likely are just jealous of your confidence and long for your freedom—so go easy on these poor souls. They just haven't found their cowgirl spirit.

Be cowgirl smart like Rose. Invent your own style and feminine identity regardless of what others think. Use your own personal style to set you apart from the competition. Here are some ideas to get you started:

1. Create your own signature satin bloomers Become known as the woman in the retro suits, stylish purses, the Greta Garbo trousers...or the kick-ass cowgirl boots. Embrace a style and be remembered for it.

2. Dress like a cowgirl. For one day, try wearing a cowboy hat and boots everywhere you go. This is particularly great on rainy days or bad-hair days. You'll find that everyone who approaches you smiles and you'll smile back—it will instantly lift your spirits. Cowboy hats also seem to make me instantly approachable. A cowboy hat is the quickest pick-me-up I know to cure a dull week. I guarantee you'll be remembered and you'll want to do it again.

3. Dress like you mean it. By wearing what you want, when you want, you'll show others that you have a cowgirl attitude of independence and self-confidence.

4. When you think you've gone too far—go further! Pull on your favorite little black dress and add an outrageous scarf, a fake-fur collar, a boa or even a well-placed fake tattoo. For a clothes-horse cowgirl, more is more.

11. Ride High in the Saddle

"Riding high in the saddle" is an Old West phrase that used to mean a cowboy was proud of his mount. Later it was used to describe someone who was happy with life. Women with cowgirl smarts ride high in the saddle because they maintain an optimistic attitude. Cowgirls find things to be happy about, even when the trail is tough and their saddle is worn.

Women who pioneered the West, whether ranching, farming or working in a mining town, had to constantly work to maintain a positive outlook. In the 1800s, there was plenty around them to bring their spirits down, and women who chose to revel in their self-pity rather than take pride in their accomplishments didn't last long. It took an unusually optimistic cowgirl to see the joy in pioneering or ranching in that vast empty terrain.

Elinore Pruitt Stewart was a remarkable pioneer whose undying optimism made her famous in 1913 after the publication of her "Letters of a Woman Homesteader" in *Atlantic Monthly*. Elinore was seen by easterners as the archetypal woman homesteader, a model for all women who wished to raise themselves out of poverty and lead a more fulfilling life. What made her eternal optimism so remarkable were the terribly difficult hardships she endured during her first thirty years of life.

Elinore was born in 1876 in the Chicka-saw Nation Indian Territory. She learned early that life would grant her no favors. Her father died when she was very young and her mother quickly remarried her husband's brother. Eli-nore had lived poor up to this point, but this new union brought eight stepbrothers and step-sisters into their home. Soon, she understood what poor *really* meant. She was never able to attend school, but she taught herself to read by picking up scraps of newspaper and asking the local storekeeper what the words meant.

When Elinore was finally able to attend school, her excitement only lasted a day, for the teacher was dragged out of the schoolroom and hanged. Shortly thereafter, her stepfather was brutally shot in their home. Elinore wrote that she was ten before she "knew that anyone could die without being shot."

Elinore took care of her brothers and sis-ters, but she unexpectedly became their guard-ian when her mother died just after Elinore's seventeenth birthday. When her stepfather passed away the next year, Elinore took five of her brothers and sisters to live with her blind grandmother, but after several years, it became too much for the old woman's health. Elinore and her siblings moved out with nothing to their names. To survive, Elinore found work on a Sante Fe Railroad construction project for herself and her three oldest siblings. The work was physically demanding and dangerous.

After two years of toiling on the railroad,

Elinore's spirits were raised when Harry Rupert, twenty-two years her senior, asked her to marry him and move to his homestead in the Indian Territory. This union only lasted four years before Elinore fled with her two sisters to Oklahoma City where Elinore gave birth to her first child. When her ex-husband threatened to take the child away, Elinore boarded a train for Denver. After thirty years of struggling to survive, Elinore found herself in a new city with no money, no job and no friends. The situation seemed so dismal that her two sisters opted to travel to California, which lessened Elinore's burden but left her with no family.

I'm sure you're thinking I've made this tale up! Where could I have found such a melancholy story? What could this possibly have to do with cowgirl smarts? I've included Elinore's past so you'll realize that her optimism later in life, was nothing short of amazing. Elinore had only seen the good life through other's living room windows and she was determined to have some for herself. She wanted to homestead on land of her own. In 1909, with nowhere else to turn, Elinore optimistically took a chance and answered a newspaper ad that read:

Wanted—Young or middle-aged lady as companion and to assist with housework on Wyoming ranch; a good permanent home for the right party.

Elinore believed in luck. She believed this opportunity was her ticket to happiness. As it turned out, she was right, but her happiness had more to do with her attitude than her new life. Clyde Stewart took Elinore from the filth of the Denver mining town to Henry's Fork, a small community in a valley just north of the Uinta Mountains in Wyoming. At thirty-three, Elinore filed on a homestead adjacent to Clyde's. When her land grant was finalized, they were married. For the first time since her mother's death, she had a home. She had struggled all her life just to survive, so the bounty of vegetables she raised in the short Wyoming summer made Henry's Fork seem like a Garden of Eden. To one of her correspondents in New England she wrote of the glories of tending gardens and cooking all day. Her letters contained descriptions of her cooking that read like sensationalized restaurant reviews. The same work other pioneers bemoaned, Elinore wrote passionately about.

When other women asked Elinore why she found the hard life of a rancher's wife so amusing, she responded, "I am a firm believer in laughter. I am real superstitious about it. I think if Bad Luck came along, he would take to his heels if someone laughed right loudly." Elinore often told others that she "could never see the good of moping." Instead, she laughed at the many mistakes she made as a "tenderfoot" in the wild. When stranded by a snowstorm, she camped under the stars and delighted in the fact that the night sky was so beautiful—she could hardly sleep. Whether broken down on a remote road or tossed from the saddle, Elinore laughed through her mishaps.

Elinore also laughed at her husband's mistakes as well. When she took a short trip to visit a Mormon settlement, her husband hired a paperhanger who had nothing under his hat but hair. The "tackler" decided to reverse every other strip of the rose-covered wallpaper so that some of the roses would grow up and some would grow down. Her reaction was typically Elinore, "A little thing like wallpaper put on upside down doesn't bother me; but what would I do if I were a 'second' [wife of a Mormon]."

The portraits of Wyoming life that Elinore painted for readers of *Atlantic Monthly* were dreamlike. In actuality, she and her family faced the same hardships common to ranchers in Wyoming—winters taking 90% of the herd, beef prices dropping as cattle reached the railhead and a constant shortage of hired hands. It wasn't that Elinore fictionalized her life in Wyoming for her readers; she believed it was a great adventure that was both rewarding and fulfilling. Her optimism lit the darkest of nights and poorest of times for her and encouraged thousands of readers that they, too, could pull themselves from desperation and live a better life.

Lessons Learned

In museums and historical societies across the West, I laughed as I thumbed through pictures of women in the 1800s making merry.

Three women in South Dakota pinned their hair to a clothesline above them, making their photo a witch-like hoot. Two women in Kansas perched in a tree like birds for a good laugh. And my favorite: two women kicking their heels together in a silhouette portrait taken atop a craggy outcrop in Yosemite Park. These women had little to entertain them, so they entertained themselves. These women knew how to ride high in the saddle.

Women with cowgirl smarts learn to make the best of every situation. I've lived most of my life, following a silly creedo: "If you're going to the party, you might as well have a good time." When most of my friends were whining about who they hated at a party, dreading how boring the party might be or threatening not to attend if they didn't know anyone, I thought they were nuts. I was glad I had an invitation, because nothing could stop me from having a good time. When I had to attend six-hour banquets in connection with my husband's office or my job required me to escort five Asian men to ride the mechanical bull at Billy Bob's, I always repeated to myself, "If you're going to the party, you might as well have a good time." It applies to almost any situation—particularly when you'd rather not be there. If you tell yourself that you'll have fun, you will—I always do, sometimes a little too much fun.

Here are some ideas for riding high in your own saddle of life:

1. Yell "yeehaw!" like you mean it. If you don't feel like belting out "yeehaw" every now and then, you're just not living. Last time I was in New York City, I got a lot of cat calls over my boots and Stetson hat. I'd return the favor by encouraging the culprit to join me in yelling yeehaw! "Say it like you mean it!" I'd demand, and they'd belt it out even louder. When possible, I'd have the whole table of Yankees yelling it. You know, I could tell it made them happy. It always does. Try it, but yell it like you mean it. Yeeeehaaaaw!

2. Savor small blessings. Enough said.

3. Find what fills your heart with joy. Have you ever known someone who can't wait to face each day even though they hate their job or their kids are making them nuts? Chances are, they've found what makes them happy and they live for that time. Whether it's reading, gardening, art or riding that gives you joy, include it in your weekly plans.

4. When the day seems impossible, turn to a cowgirl friend for help. Sometimes a wise woman's advice and a margarita can be just the pick-me-up you need.

5. Choose to be positive. "Well duh!" you say. Sure it's the oldest advice in the book. It's overused because it's true. You always have the choice to evaluate any situation as negative or positive—the facts don't change, just your attitude toward them. When the rodeo of life is bucking particularly hard, a positive attitude will save you like a pick-up man in a bronc ride.

6. Accept the past and move on. On a ranch, horses die, favorite dogs get trampled and an early frost ruins your winter hay. Cowgirls learn to mourn and move on. You have to believe tomorrow is better, or it won't be.

12. Ride High,
But Stay Grounded

Riding high in the saddle is a great way to go through life, but it's important to temper that feeling by being authentic. Being an authentic cowgirl isn't about having manure on your boots; it's about being genuine and honest; it's about being a realist.

When I interviewed Helen Groves – the First Lady of Cutting and a Cowgirl Hall of Fame Inductee – for my book, I asked her, "What makes cowgirls successful?" She promptly told me that it was their ability to be real. That may sound like one simple word to describe cowgirls, but for Helen it has many deep and powerful meanings.

In the 1920s and 1930s, when Helen was growing up on the legendary King Ranch in Texas, she learned at an early age that cowgirls have to face the realities of life—animals die, but others are born to replace them, droughts are horrible, but there's always an end. Helen recalled the Easter morning when the barn cats killed her new Easter bunny. Her parents didn't try to hide it from her; instead, they looked at the incident as real life and taught Helen to accept reality as a way to keep riding high in her saddle.

Cowgirls don't ride through life giving the

false impression that everything will always be hunky-dory, nor do they expect it to be. I'm sure you have some girlfriends that when asked how they are, will always respond, "Great!" —even when they aren't. Telling friends that you're riding high in the saddle, when in actuality you're not, isn't authentic or honest. Making yourself appear to be something you are not will also decrease others' trust in you. Cowgirls don't twist a friend's ear off by dwelling on their problems, but they always remain real to their friends.

Helen is a very optimistic woman, but she's learned to be careful about who and what she trusts. "Don't pick up a rat by the tail in order to save it from the cat," said Helen. "The rat will bite you, and the cat won't appreciate it either." Cowgirls like Helen learn to face the unfortunate reality that not all things or people can be trusted. In the real world, many people won't be as genuine and honest as you are. The goal is not only to stay optimistic, but to stay grounded as well.

For Helen, being real also means being a genuine friend. She looks after her cowgirl companions on the trail and never leaves the roundup until the last calf is branded and all are mothered up. Helen is one heck of a competitive rider, but she approaches each new event not only wanting to win, but also looking for ways she can contribute. She's nationally known as the First Lady of Cutting in recognition for both her achievements and her contributions to the cutting horse industry. But even at the top of her game, she never shirks a request to help out others coming up in the ranks of cutting. That's what genuine cowgirls do.

Being real also means accepting that there will always be cowgirls who are better than you. If you always think you're the best rider on the ranch, you're headed for a painful fall from the saddle. While Helen thinks competition is great, she's against raising children to believe that everyone is a winner. "You have to learn to accept and respect others who are better than you," says Helen. "If I'm not as smart as them, then maybe I can learn something from them." That's a mighty big statement coming from a woman as competent and wise as Helen. Being real means knowing your strengths and weaknesses and when to use them to your advantage. It's like a quail who escapes the claws of a hawk—not because he's faster, but because he's more clever.

Probably the most difficult dose of reality Helen ever faced was to have to sell the King Ranch. In 2003, the King Ranch celebrated its 150th anniversary. You can imagine how her heart sank at the thought of not being the sole owner of this impressive distinction. She remembers her childhood on the ranch with her favorite Shetland pony—one day she'd ride him like a cutting horse; the next day she'd brush his teeth when they played doctor. When she was feeling feisty, she'd pinch her pony's butt and make him prance like a circus horse on his hind legs. That pony is just one of the many fond memories she has of growing up on her beloved ranch.

While reflecting on the loss of her childhood ranch, Helen said, "I have to look at things like they are, not like I want them to be." It's a great lesson for all cowgirls—to keep it real, be authentic, and most of all, be genuine.

Lessons Learned:

1. Be honest and genuine. This is fundamental to living the cowgirl way and it's one of the most important points in the Cowgirl Creed. Start by being honest with yourself. Are you projecting the real cowgirl inside? If not, it probably shows. Living an unauthentic life will wear you down and make it difficult to rope a kick-ass life.

2. Be a realist. Take some sage advice from Helen Groves, "You have to look at things like they are, not how you want them to be." This doesn't mean giving up or accepting that you'll never be as good as your mentor. Earning the all-round cowgirl title in whatever you aspire to be requires a careful assessment of your strengths and weaknesses so you can develop a foolproof trail map for achieving your goals. Winning doesn't come easily; there are just some people who make it look that way.

3. Keep a realistic view. Life is like the rhythm of a ranch: some things die but others are born to take their place. Accept that things will not always go your way, and you'll handle disappointment better. Quickly bouncing back from life's disappointments will keep you riding high in the saddle for more days than your thighs and butt can take.

4. Don't live your life to please others. When you live your life to please others, you're likely trying to be someone you aren't. We all want to please our parents, but if being authentic means loosening the apron strings, then learn to do it diplomatically. You can respect others and still be your own cowgirl.

5. Life's not fair. This was my mother's standard remark, when as a young child I complained that my older brothers got something that I did not. I still repeat those words today, more often than I'd like. You must learn to accept the injustices in life and use your cowgirl smarts to cleverly overcome them. If you throw yourself a pity party, you'll be the life of your party, but you won't have a very good time.

6. Let your passion show. As an executive and consultant in high-tech marketing, I was always afraid to let my love for riding and cowgirls show. Black silk suits and a laptop weren't the real me—I'd rather have been in chaps snapping a quirt. When I started wearing boots with suits and letting my passion show, I found the business world admired me for the dichotomy of my interests and the passion to follow my heart.

I'm now a cowgirl of my convictions. Be real and let your passion show.

13. Give Others a Leg Up

When I first went horseback riding, I was approached by a woman wrangler who offered, "Let me give you a leg up." Did I look like I needed help getting into the saddle? My independent spirit quickly responded, "I think I can manage, thank you." Wrong answer! The cowgirl way is to help other cowgirls. Cowgirls on the ground always offer to give others a leg up. The rider graciously accepts help, but puts as little weight on the supported leg as possible. The leg up is only there if you need it.

Early cowgirls competing in a man's world not only stuck together, they helped each other learn the ropes. Cowgirl stories are filled with generous gestures of physical, emotional and financial support. These women gave a leg up to their companions and competitors alike. No one was better known for this than Lucille Mulhall, who grew up working on the 101 Ranch, home of one of the most famous Wild West shows. She worked with a team of cowboys who mentored and encouraged her until she was one of the best ropers and riders in the country. Life on the 101 Ranch engrained in her a deep appreciation for always helping other riders.

In 1916, the Royal American Stock Show in Kansas City, Missouri, made a big advertisement for its trick riding contest. Unfortunately, only two women entered the trick riding contest and the contest had to have three contestants or it would be cancelled. Lucille was friends with the only two entrants: Mayme Stroud and Babe Willetts. To assist her friends, Lucille loaned her steady horse, White Man, to newcomer, Mildred Douglas. Being a bull and bronc rider, Mildred didn't know anything about trick riding. Lucille taught Mildred a few tricks before the contest and even coached her during the competition by telling her what to do each time she circled the arena. Lucille's teaching paid off for Mildred, but not so well for Babe. Mayme won first and Mildred placed a very respectful second.

Mildred later recalled Lucille's generosity not only to herself, but to other contestants as well. Lucille often roped and snubbed broncs for her competitors and never turned them loose until the cowgirl gave her the call to "let 'er buck." Many wondered why she so often helped other cowgirls competing against her. Lucille knew that more cowgirls not only made for a better show, but kept her working to be a better cowgirl contestant.

Lucille was one confident cowgirl with tons of cowgirl smarts. She was long referred to as Queen of the Cowgirls. Her abilities and accomplishments have rarely been matched even in today's professional rodeo circuit.

Another cowgirl who knew how to give others a leg up was Fox Hastings, one of the best trick riders on the circuit. In 1925, Geneva "Gene" Kreig was new to the rodeo circuit. She had earned a substantial sum riding broncs at the Cheyenne Frontier Days and at the Chicago Round-Up. But rodeo promoters needed women who could enter multiple events and Gene was a one-trick-pony. When the Pendleton Round-Up needed trick riders, Fox took Gene under her wing, found her a steady trick horse and taught her to trick ride. With the help of a great teacher and friend, Gene went on to compete against Fox for almost fifteen years until Gene was injured in 1940 at the Madison Square Gardens Rodeo. Fox truly knew the meaning of giving a friend a leg up.

In the 1920s, the cowgirl stars of Madison Square Gardens were as glamorous as they were physically strong. While their elaborate sequin-covered costumes displayed their feminine side, these cowgirls were clearly a different breed of women who lived by a different standard—that of fierce independence. Women wearing sequins, but with more strength than many men and a lifestyle that resembled the toughest cowboy, seemed a dichotomy to the flappers and sexist men of the times. These cowgirls provided new examples of a woman's potential. They inspired women of eastern society to have new dreams and ambitions.

With their growing popularity on the East Coast, cowgirls became the symbol for independence and confidence. Manufacturers began using cowgirls in their advertising to attract free thinking women—and it goes without saying that it attracted more than a few men as well. Many historians and sociologists claim that what makes American women so different from other nationalities is their role models from the West. Unknowingly, cowgirls gave their East Coast sisters a leg up in becoming the quintessential Americana woman—a fact some men loved and others loathed.

Lessons Learned

It's cowgirl smart to give other women a leg up, but you'll want to give your kids a leg up too. Cowgirls have a unique way of passing cowgirl smarts to their own children. Today's ranch women aren't that different from the earliest ranch mothers who settled the West. The ranching life demands a lot of a woman. Long days filled with chores end only hours before they begin again. Given the environment, ranch children must learn to be independent and self-sufficient at an early age. Before their teens, they take on responsibilities that affect the welfare of the livestock as well as the ranch family. Ranchers give their kids a leg up by engraining in them a strong work ethic and a clear understanding of responsibility.

Parents can't *give* cowgirl smarts to their children. No one can. To gain a sense of accomplishment and learn personal pride, a child must do for herself. When kids carve out their own trail, especially when the terrain is difficult, they feel a sense of accomplishment and their confidence grows. The very act of blazing your own trail is what builds strength of character and ultimately helps you discover what you want out of life. But to give your child a leg up doesn't mean holding their hand all the way down the trail. Both confidence and personal pride are built when your child looks back down the trail, sees how far she's come, and knows she did it for herself, by herself. Funny, it's kind of an oxymoron: cowgirls give their children a leg up by knowing when to stand back.

Here are some Cowgirl Smarts ideas for helping you practice giving others a leg up.

1. Embrace other cowgirls One of the places I hate the most is the women's restrooms in bars. I'd rather join the men. Women seem to love to talk trash about other women; and give a woman a drink and the talk never stops. I remember Oprah once challenged her viewers to go an entire week without saying anything bad about someone else. More than half the women admitted they couldn't do it. You have to get your mind set that other women are your teammates and not your enemy. How would your life improve if you helped the women around you and they all improved? You'd be challenged and your life would be richer for it.

2. Don't make your success dependent on others' failure. I once had a friend who always said, "It isn't enough that I succeed, all others must fail." Gasp! That is what's wrong with half the workplaces I've been in. We all need to learn to help others and view them as cowgirls on the same trail ride.

3. Remember that city slickers have a cowgirl spirit too. If you're a real cowgirl, understand that you have a gift that you can share with city slickers everywhere. Don't be proud or pompous; instead, share your cowgirl smarts. If those city slickers put you down at first, be generous and give them a second chance. They are no different than the horses pulling carts in New York City...their spirit has been broken for a long time, but it's still there. Encourage them to run through a grassy pasture filled with wildflowers and their spirit will emerge anew.

4. Cowgirl Up and Pass it Down. Your children learn by your example, but they learn even more by doing for themselves. Think like a cowgirl and give your kids more responsibilities. Find an activity where their participation affects the family and let them feel needed. Assign truly difficult tasks so they feel a true sense of accomplishment. Know you'll first have to undo the lessons they learn in school where everyone is a winner. In real life, some kids blaze their own trail and fail. It's the process of learning to cowgirl up by getting back on the horse that will build lasting confidence.

14. Always Get Back On the Horse

Failure isn't about being bucked off the horse. It's about getting back on. When you get thrown, you can choose to walk away and decide that riding isn't for you, or you can pop your foot in the stirrup and climb back on. The horse will respect you for it, and you'll learn to respect yourself more, too.

Cowgirls know a lot about getting bucked off—not just by horses, but by life, too. No one ever chooses to be a cowgirl because it's easy. The job is filled with hard knocks from sick cattle to unstable beef prices. Through long droughts, the price of hay will double or triple, while the price for cattle will plummet. When there's finally enough rain, the wind won't blow, so your windmills can't pump the water from the ground. Then there are the long hours, working seven days a week, trying to find the energy to work the next day after being up all night with a mare giving birth or catching collecting newborn calves before they freeze in the snow. Ask any cowgirl and she'll tell you that foaling problems never seem to happen during daylight hours.

Even when these cowgirls play nursemaid all night, they still have a full day of chores come daybreak. Fact is, ranching is one of the toughest and lowest paying jobs around. But

119

cowgirls don't do it for the money. They become cowgirls because they love the work and they've learned to always get back on the horse when life bucks them off.

As hard as today's ranching may be, it doesn't compare to the hardships families faced trying to establish ranches across the West in the 1800s. You can pick up any pioneering history book and be astounded at what our ancestors were willing to sacrifice for economic freedom. One of my favorite pioneering stories is about a cowgirl named Ben McCulloch, or Flapper Fannie as she was known. Fannie was a Texas cowgirl with a spirit that wouldn't stop.

Fannie was born in Whitesboro, Texas, in 1862 and the very next year, her father moved the family to a 1000-acre ranch on the Red and Little Wichita Rivers where their cattle could roam the free grazing lands. Her father also bought six large farms and planted orchards that were the first in that region of Texas. Whether Fannie got her entrepreneurial talent genetically or from working with her father, it was clear from an early age that she would be a successful cattlewoman. Here's how Fannie described getting her first start in the cattle business.

One day during a roundup, the cowboys found a fawn. It was so cunning they brought it to me. This was my favorite pet. I would sleep and eat with it. I was about eight years old, and we had great romps together. When spring came my fawn had grown and was very destructive to the orchard. One morning father said, 'Ben, I'd like to swap you out of that deer.' I said, 'What have you got?' He said, 'I'll trade you that little speckled heifer for him.' I agreed, of course, because I thought I would get to romp with the deer anyway, but no, father sent me away for a few days and when I returned; my deer had been killed and most of it eaten. The next morning I went out to the hay stack and my heifer had a little calf, the blackest little devil you ever saw. This was how I got my start in the cattle business.

To raise money for additional calves, Fannie began peddling fruit. She would gather fruit from her father's orchards and take it to town where a friendly, old judge would help her sell it. From these small fruit sales she saved her nickels and dimes. Each time she had enough money, she'd buy a dogie (a motherless calf) because they were cheap and she knew dogies would have more calves. To add to her herd, she would also ride the range, cutting out unbranded cattle. By the time she was seventeen years old, she was buying and selling cattle like a man.

In 1881, when Fannie was nineteen, she married W. A. Miskimon and moved to Jacks County, Texas. She brought to the marriage a sizable herd of cattle and property. But she soon found that her husband knew as much about

121

cattle as a hog does a sidesaddle. To make matters worse, she could only count on one thing in Texas—brutal weather and hard knocks. Even with good cowhands, Texas herds were lost faster than they were raised. Here's how Fannie described her first years of marriage and living on her own.

> We lived in Jack County seventeen miles below Jacksboro. We had a mighty hard time, lots of cattle, and dry weather. My husband wasn't no cowman, I tried to teach him about cows but he never could learn, not even feed one. At last God gave me a boy. We would have to stay by ourselves on many instances. Once, my husband went to Missouri on business. The severe drought had caused all the water holes to sink and all wells to dry up. I strapped the baby on my back, papoose style, and would walk a mile or two for water. The wild hogs rooted in the low places, and water would come up in small holes. With my baby on my back and a tea cup in my hand I would dip water here and there until I filled my buckets and carry the weary load home. The people of today demand water in the house or will not rent. I didn't stay out of the saddle long. I began riding the range again when my baby (papoose, I called him) was quite small.

Nine years later, in 1889, Fannie and her husband moved to San Angelo, Texas, where water was plentiful and there were more open ranges for free grazing. Prior to crossing the Brazos, Fannie and her five hired hands from Mexico bedded down the cattle for the night, intending to push them across the river at daybreak. The skies poured buckets that night and her hired hands began to shiver with fevers from years of battling malaria. While trying to keep a fire going for her cowhands, Fannie found herself alone and trying to hold her herd together while wolves howled and panthers screamed. She remembers it as one of the scariest nights of her life. After that harrowing night, most women would have thought twice about moving their cattle with just a few ranch hands, but not Fannie.

Fannie continued to roundup her own cattle, and soon Fannie's herd and pocketbook grew. In 1893, she bought out a local rancher and all his cattle. Her herd was so large at that point, that she found herself riding and roping more than most men. But like all ranchers in the 1800s, her prosperity was at the mercy of the elements. In 1894, a severe drought left her cattle as gaunt as gutted snowbirds. They were starving for water and food. With no rain for nine months, Fannie's cattle died by the hundreds each day. She felt like a frazzled rope ready to snap. When all seemed lost, it got worse. The bank repossessed her ranch.

Most cowgirls, who found themselves in Fannie's position, would have given up, but not Fannie. When ranch life bucked her off, she got back on the only horse that paid—retail. With a ninety-day loan, Fannie opened a dress and millinery shop in San Angelo. In those days, prostitutes were the biggest buyers of ladies wear, but brothels were in a restricted district where women of her class weren't allowed on the streets. To turn a fast profit, Fannie used her cowgirl smarts. She hired a young negro boy as her courier. He would take dress designs and sample fabrics to the prostitutes and take their orders for dresses, hats and parasols. The prostitutes, also known as soiled doves, appreciated a store that catered to their needs and their money was good as gold. In ninety days, she raised enough money to buy back her ranch from the same bankers who disdained the red-light district. (Don't you know Fannie had a good laugh over that?)

With $500 earned from dress sales and $300 earned from selling her store to a local merchant, she got her ranch out of debt. With the drought over and her ranch back, she began rebuilding her herd. Though short of ranch hands, Fannie used her cowgirl smarts to work her cattle. She opened her ranch to all passing cowboys and served them boiled beef, red beans and coffee in return for rounding-up her cattle before moving on.

At seventy-three years of age, Fannie was still riding strong. Here's how she described her life to a writer for the Federal Writers Project:

I've had many trials and tribulations, but

*I own a good country home now and lots of
chickens and stock, four lots in Westland
Park, and all the west end of block P on
West College Avenue. My one daughter,
her husband, and children are here with
me. I am about as happy as most people
of my age. I'm still working hard as a
cowman for my husband, 'cause I've tried
for 54 years to teach him, and he has never
yet learned. He never will as long as my
name is Ben McCulloch Earl Van Dorn
Miskimon.*

When life yelled, "Buck off!" Fannie
always climbed back on. She was never beat-
en—not by a horse, a drought, a banker or even
a husband that never learned to help with the
ranch. She was truly cowgirl smart.

Another cowgirl who really knew how
to recover from a bad ride was Maxine from
Lewiston, Idaho. Maxine was a rodeo princess
in 1936 at the Lewiston Round Up in Idaho.
Although Maxine grew up on a ranch and could
ride with the best of them, she was limited to
the only rodeo event in Lewiston still left for
women—the rodeo court, made up of a queen
and two princesses.

Being a rodeo princess was flattering, but
Maxine wanted to perform like the cowboys.
Maxine was looking for a good bronc ride to dem-
onstrate her cowgirl skill. When the Lewiston
Round Up had ended for the day, Maxine was
hoping to try out the bucking stock. Thinking

125

he was doing Maxine a favor, her brother Russ determined that Maxine could ride an unbroken horse named Raleigh a lot more safely than one of the broncs from the rough rodeo stock. With cowboys still hanging on the arena fence, her brother brought Raleigh into the arena and wrestled the horse to the ground, hobbling the horse as they did at some rodeos instead of using chutes. This act alone of hobbling the horse had generated an audience of some of the best cowboys at the round up. Russ told Maxine that this was her big chance to show them what cowgirls were made of.

With the horse still hobbled by ropes, Russ yelled for Maxine to jump in the saddle and whip the horse for the ride of her life. Eager to work a bucking horse in front of real rodeo professionals, Maxine jumped on the horse, pulled down her hat and wrapped her hand tightly around the saddle horn. When Maxine was ready, she ordered Russ to let her buck. With ropes flying, the horse sprang to its feet. But instead of bucking, the horse just stood there and proceeded to fart and fart and make other unseemly noises. Still farting, it slowing swaggered down the arena with Maxine on top looking like a cowgirl on a mechanical horse that someone forgot to feed another nickel. Maxine clearly yelled "Let 'er Buck, but this horse must have heard "Let 'er Rip."

The cowboys all roared with laughter. Here she was poised to make her rodeo dream come true, and all she got was a horse with gas.

Maxine's big chance to bronc ride at the rodeo ended in disappointment. Maxine may not have physically gotten bucked from her horse, but her pride had taken a serious beating. Being cowgirl smart, Maxine made the best of it by laughing with the cowboys and by entertaining dozens of friends with this hilarious tale for over sixty years.

Lessons Learned

Getting back on the horse that bucked you off is one of the toughest life lessons. I've helped young girls and women alike who were literally bucked off a horse, gather their courage months later after their bones had healed and get back on to ride again. I've been there myself, both literally and figuratively. I've found the sooner you get back on and overcome your fear, the easier it will be. And afterwards, you will wonder why it took you so long.

There are several important lessons you can learn from Fannie and Maxine about overcoming bad knocks in life and they equally apply when you've made personal mistakes that you need to overcome:

1. Failure is a test of spirit, not a reason to give up. My mother always used the quote, "That which doesn't kill us, makes us stronger." There's a lot of wisdom in those words. I rode out the harder trails in life by reminding myself of this. When you look back at the tough times in your life, identify how they made you a better woman. Accept failure as a lesson in riding the rodeo of life.

2. When cow poking doesn't pay, find another way. If you lose your job, your house or even your ranch, use all the talents God gave you to win it back. That might mean changing gears and taking a less desirable job until you get back on your feet. Remember that cowgirls are never too proud to cut and haul hay when cows don't pay. Do what you have to do to pay the bills. Be sure your pride doesn't cause you to forfeit what you love the most.

3. No one ever notices how you ride until you fall off. That's because failure isn't about falling off, it's about getting back on. Watch a dude ranch wrangler. When a city slicker falls off, they size up the gal by how quickly she gets back on. When life seems to be yelling "buck off," gather your courage and get back on.

4. Laughter is the best bandage for a bruised pride. All of us, at one time or another, fail in front of our family or peers. Most people react with anger, but women with cowgirl smarts learn to confront defeat with laughter. Watch cowgirls at a rodeo. When a cowgirl draws a bad horse or a lame calf, their buddies will make a joke. The smart cowgirl will laugh with them. It's the best medicine when you get the short end of the stick.

15. Ride Beside Your Man

In the 1800s, eastern women and men lived in separate worlds. While women were confined to domestic chores and socials, men lived largely in politics and the business world. Women weren't seen as equals in work or vote, so most men felt no obligation to treat them as such. On the frontier, ranches were always short of hands. Anyone who could rope and ride was considered a cowboy equal, regardless of gender or age. For this reason, many cowboys saw women as equals long before our Eastern sisters had that same privilege. When western women asked for the vote, cowboys only thought it fair to give it to them. This is why women in many western states were given the right to vote, 13 years before their eastern sisters.

Women in the East didn't understand their western sisters. Frequently, pioneer women would receive letters of sympathy from family back East, who pitied the woman who had to ride beside her man. Amanda Burks, a Texas cowgirl who rode the Chisholm Trail with her husband in 1871, wrote this response to a sympathetic letter from a friend back East.

"What woman, youthful and full of spirit and the love of living, needs sympathy because of availing herself of the opportunity of being with her husband while at his chosen work in the great out-

of-door world?"

It was a stunning declaration at the time, for few women chose physical labor over a retired society life.

With women riding beside their husbands across the West, it's not surprising that they approached marriage differently than their eastern counterparts. Most western women and men saw marriage as a partnership. However, when a man expected his wife to work along side him, but not be treated equally, he frequently found his bed empty and divorce papers served shortly thereafter. Cowgirls would ride beside their men to hell and back, but only if he respected her in the voting booth and in marriage. In Montana from 1865 to 1870, there was one divorce for every three marriages, but the divorce rate soon plummeted. It seems Montana cowgirls taught men to ride beside their women or to go without.

A great example of a husband-and-wife partnership can be seen in Mr. and Mrs. Jack Miles who lived in San Angelo, Texas, in the 1800s. In her senior years, Ms. Miles told a writer from the Federal Writers Project about the thrilling adventures she had riding, cowboying and foxhunting with her husband.

> *"Few women in the entire history of the cow country ever threw their sugins [bedding] in the wagon and rode the range with their husband like a man as I did," said Mrs. Miles. "I certainly enjoyed ranch life and*

wish I could live it all over again."

Mrs. Miles' father-in-law owned three of the largest ranches in West Texas and her husband Jack managed them all. She worked months in the saddle with her husband rounding up and branding cattle. "I can rope a streak of lightning and ride it where I please," she once bragged. She went on cattle drives and after bringing in the herd, she threw her share of calves to be branded. She and her husband even chased and roped wild Mustangs together:

> *The hardest ride I ever made was after a big mustang horse. He was a beautiful creature with long silken mane and tail. Jack and I captured several of them. This one got with an old outlaw horse that had on a big bell. We knew we would have to run him down to catch him, so we started toward the ranch. We ran them about fifteen miles and the clang of that big bell got louder and louder. I can hear it yet, when I think of that ride. We captured the old rascal about sundown. I didn't have a dry thread on me.*

The only inequality between Mrs. Miles and her cowboy partner was that she had her own tent which the cook always pitched for her—more out of respect than necessity. But when it came to taking shifts holding the herd at night or holding the cutouts at bay, Mrs. Miles carried her share of the work and made a good hand. She truly knew the meaning of riding beside her partner. Her marriage and her life were better for it.

A more famous cowgirl, whom I'm sure you've heard of, had an extraordinary business partnership with Buffalo Bill. However, few knew the remarkable partnership Annie Oakley had with her husband Frank Butler. Frank was a sharpshooter like Annie. The two met when Frank was traveling with an act that invited people in her town to try and out-shoot the expert marksman. Annie challenged Frank and beat him in his own show. This unusual show of dominance fascinated Frank and after several months of courting, he asked Annie to marry him.

Initially, Frank and Annie performed as a team, but when Frank realized Annie had much more potential than he ever hoped to have, he stepped down from the act, but never left her side. In an era when husbands were bread-winners and wives were subservient, Frank's actions were commendable. With Frank as her husband, manager and favorite hunting partner, Annie appreciated a husband who would ride beside her, not in front.

Another notable sharpshooter who stood by her man was May Lillie, wife of Pawnee Bill. May was the daughter of a Quaker physician and a graduate of Smith College. She seemed an unlikely mate for this wild man who lived with Indians and entertained friends by drinking cow blood. In her first year of marriage, May stayed home being the dutiful housewife. Soon she was pregnant. Unfortunately she had a difficult child birth requiring an operation that left her unable to bare children. To make matters worse, her only child died six weeks later. With motherhood no longer an option, May threw herself into her husband's world by joining her husband's Wild West show.

Through daily practice, May became an expert sharpshooter. Riding, roping and shooting was a far cry from her Quaker upbringing and an even further leap from her intellectual studies. Nonetheless, May rode by her husband inside and outside the show arena. She was billed as "Princess of the Prairie" or "The New Rifle Queen," and she soon became a famous star on the Wild West show circuit.

May was well known for riding beside her man, but became even more famous for knowing when to refuse to ride beside him. Buffalo Bill's Wild West Show was Pawnee Bill's inspiration for starting his own show—he admired, even adored, Buffalo Bill. So when Pawnee Bill was offered the chance to buy an interest in Buffalo Bill's show and merge their two shows, he couldn't resist. May vehemently opposed the merger because their own show now had a good following and she knew Buffalo Bill was a poor business manager. May knew the merger would cripple their business. She told her husband that if he insisted on the merger, he'd have to do it without her. He was a hard man to change so May left Pawnee Bill's side and returned to their ranch outside Pawnee, Oklahoma. Only four years later, in 1913, the two Bills claimed bankruptcy and the curtain came down on the "Two-Bill Show." Meanwhile their competitors from the 101 Ranch had their best season ever.

With their ranch still in tack, May forgave Pawnee Bill and welcomed him home. She later wrote, "Time smoothes everything." May stood her ground for what she knew was right. Her husband clearly had a lapse in good judgment, but she forgave him, just as he forgave her for not staying by his side. Through their retirement years, May and Pawnee Bill rode their ranch side by side, hunting, fishing and occasionally roping a stray cow or two. May was cowgirl smart in refusing to support a flawed business plan, but even smarter to forgive her husband's transgression.

Lessons Learned

To ride beside your man, you don't have to actually take up riding (although I highly recommend it as a sport for couples). Mrs. Miles, Annie and May literally did ride beside their men, but the point of their stories is that they viewed marriage as a partnership. Each of these couples worked to further each other's careers and acted as advisors when necessary. These wives didn't try to run their husband's lives; they learned to take part as equals.

I've known a few cowgirls who never learned how to ride beside their men—they preferred to ride their backs. They thought they could treat men like horses—first breaking them and then training them to respond to the slightest command. Fact is, men aren't like horses. You can't watch their cars to tell how they feel. If you insist on treating men like horses, they will act like horses by biting, bucking or breaking away—for good reason, too. Treating men like horses just isn't cowgirl smart.

Real cowgirls ride beside their man, treating them as equals and expecting nothing less in return. Here are a few pointers on riding beside your man:

1. Be your pardner's best friend. I was lucky enough to marry my best friend. Our partnership was formed long before our vows. If you and your man weren't best friends before your marriage, it may take time to cultivate. It's a matter of building trust and enjoying your time together—same as with your best girlfriend. Work together to identify activities you both enjoy and make time to do them together. If you find you're treating your girlfriend better than your pardner, you haven't learned to ride side-by-side.

2. Be patient, good partnerships take time. It takes time to build total trust and work to maintain it. Don't walk out at the first transgression, but do stand your ground. If you find your man is horribly wrong, take a lesson from May Lillie: tell your man that you're forced to dismount your horse, but you'll keep the saddle warm for when he changes his ways.

3. Give as much as you expect to get. If you expect your man to sit through chick flicks, you'd better be able to stomach Arnold Schwarzenegger's action movies. A partnership is about taking turns.

4. Learn to forgive. We're always tempted to say "I told you so!" and sometimes pointing that out gently is educational for a hard-headed man. But be sure to always forgive first.

5. Throw a loop and gather him close. Make your man your confidant. Share your dreams and hopes and encourage him to share his as well. And remember, snuggling close isn't always about you, you, you. Sometimes, it's about him, him, him.

6. Reversed roles shouldn't change your riding style. If you're the breadwinner and your husband stays home with the kids, be careful not to run out front on the trail. Riding too far out front and rarely looking back, leaves your husband wondering just who he's riding the trail with. Be smart and let him lead the trail ride occasionally. We all like to be in charge—so take turns.

16. Recharge Your Cowgirl Spirit

All work and no play is not the cowgirl way. Women with cowgirl smarts understand the importance of recharging their cowgirl spirit. Most cowgirls let the land rejuvenate their spirit. They find solace in the open air where nature speaks to their heart. This is a characteristic that is prominent in almost all cowgirls. Whether in the mountains, the valleys, the vast deserts or the oceans' shores, cowgirls find that communing with nature calms their soul and restores the fire that drives them. Modern cow girls who find themselves walled in by cement cities, where the only livestock is the rat race, rush to the great outdoors at every opportunity. For only in the company of nature can they clear their heads and recharge themselves to fight the daily grind of city life.

Born in 1897, Hallie Crawford Stillwell was raised in West Texas as a southern lady. At nineteen, Hallie told her parents that she was moving to Presidio, Texas, a rough town on the Mexican border where she planned to teach school. Her father wouldn't hear of it. He thought it was no place for a lady. He told her, "I think you're going on a wild goose chase," to which Hallie replied, "Then I'll gather my geese." She armed herself with a six-shooter and headed for Presidio. Like her father predicted, Presidio was a rough town, but Hallie reveled in the beauty of the open West Texas land. A year later, in 1917, Hallie moved a short distance to Marathon where the dangers were fewer, but the Rocky Mountains still touched her soul.

In Marathon, Hallie met Roy Stillwell, a local rancher who shared her love for the dry West Texas land. They married and Hallie spent a lifetime ranching the desolate lands around Big Bend, Texas. As a tribute to overcoming her father's predilection, she titled her autobiography, *I'll Gather My Geese*. In her autobiography, Hallie described the daily stress and mishaps of learning to be a cowgirl among seasoned cowboys. When she felt particularly defeated, or had sorrow from the loss of a ranch animal, she'd perch upon her favorite rock outside her back door where she would watch the sunset and the birds fly overhead. It settled her mind and rejuvenated her spirit. It was a quiet commune with nature that had powerful results. The silence on that rock was profound.

Another pastime that brightened Hallie's spirits was climbing through caves and river beds near her ranch searching for Indian artifacts. Seeking the isolation from the "modern" world of 1919, coupled with her search for history, helped her commune with the land that she loved. Though the cowboys on her ranch thought her arrowhead searches were either a way to shirk work or possibly a momentary loss of mind, she persevered. To Hallie, her history-hunting expeditions were as much about nature's tranquility as they were about the search for artifacts. Her joy of discovery was finding her inner cowgirl spirit.

Then and now, many visitors to the dry lands of West Texas find it dreadfully barren and lonely. But to Hallie, the roughness of the rock and the scrub brush were a thing of beauty. Her love of the land inspired Hallie to spend much of her later years writing and teaching about the history of the area and working to preserve the land that is now Big Bend National Park. In what others deemed a God-forsaken desert, Hallie lived to be ninety-nine years old. I believe it was the land and her love for it that recharged her cowgirl spirit and kept her cowgirl smart, until she rode her last horse.

Like Hallie, lots of city slicker gals have found their cowgirl spirit on the range. One of my favorite modern city slicker cowgirls who headed west was Gretel Ehrlich, a superb film director who found that the cowgirl lifestyle made her a superb writer. She is one of my favorite cowgirl authors. She went to Wyoming in 1976 to rest her cowgirl spirit, but instead found that it had never been awakened. This is how she describes the revelation of finding her cowgirl spirit in her book, *The Solace of Open Spaces*:

> *I came here four years ago. I had not planned to stay, but I couldn't make myself leave. John, the sheepman, put me to work*

immediately. It was spring, and shearing time. For fourteen days of fourteen hours each, we moved thousands of sheep through sorting corrals to be sheared, branded, and deloused. I suspect that my original motive for coming here was to "lose myself" in new and unpopulated territory. Instead, of producing the numbness I thought I wanted, life on the sheep ranch woke me up. The vitality of the people I was working with flushed out what had become a hallucinatory rawness inside me. I threw away my clothes and bought new ones; I cut my hair. The arid country was a clean slate. Its absolute indifference steadied me.

Every woman longs to answer the calling of her cowgirl spirit. Even women in cities where the only horses are pulling carriages for tourists have cowgirl spirits—it just manifests itself differently. Your cowgirl spirit is that inner voice that wants to feel freedom, to be independent, to attain fulfillment and to ride high in the saddle. Some women hear the voice louder and more often than others do. Some women intentionally drown out the voice, because they feel they can't sacrifice what they do for others in order to fulfill themselves.

Hollywood knows we want to revive our inner cowgirl spirit. Movies like *City Slickers* and *The Horse Whisperer* whet our appetite for the cowgirl dream, even if only for a few hours.

I remember seeing *The Horse Whisperer* with a friend one night. We had both climbed the corporate ladder, only to find the view from the top was not what we expected. Our cowgirl smarts had gotten us to the top of that ladder, but the price we paid was the breaking of our cowgirl spirit. We were fed up with the corporate backstabbing and we related all too well to the movie's heroine who left her executive position in New York to find her cowgirl spirit in Montana. We spent hours after that movie discussing our plans to quit our jobs and head West. We knocked back martinis, longing for the cowgirl spirit that we didn't have the guts to grab. We felt like young girls in our first pair of pink cowboy boots, begging Mom to put one more quarter in the mechanical horse outside the Piggly Wiggly.

I never forgot that night, and it was only months later I quit the job I had always wanted and exchanged it for life on my own terms back in Texas. *The Horse Whisperer* is a tear jerker, but I highly recommend it. It's just the kick-in-the-pants many of us need to search for a better life that allows us to keep our cowgirl spirit alive. I might add, watching Robert Redford in tight blue jeans on a Montana landscape will also do wonders for recharging your cowgirl spirit.

The mistake I made was to let my company crush my cowgirl spirit. Not only did I neglect to recharge my cowgirl spirit, I let someone else extinguish it. From the outside, people thought I had an enviable executive position. On the inside I was dieing. My solution was radical—I left my job and started my own consulting company—but yours doesn't have to be. Use your cowgirl smarts to find activities that rejuvenate your cowgirl spirit.

Lessons Learned

Everyone refuels their cowgirl spirit through different activities. I fuel mine through riding, swimming and outdoor adventure trips. My cowgirl heroines recharged their souls by immersing themselves in the beauty of the land and working with animals. You may find that the down time and pampering a spa offers works wonders. Finding your cowgirl spirit can be as simple as pulling on a new pair of cowgirl boots—they always make me stand a little taller, walk a little more boldly and sass a little louder. Add a cowboy hat and you'll hardly be able to control yourself—I know I can't.

An important precursor to recharging your spirit is shedding your stress, even if only for a few hours or a day. For many of us, clearing our mind requires putting the past behind us and moving on. When I left my executive job, I found I couldn't enjoy my new freedom until I analyzed my mistakes and moved on. I kept kicking myself for wanting something so badly that I was willing to relinquish my spirit. I never wanted that to happen again. Once I forgave myself, my cowgirl spirit was restored and I was riding the high road again.

Women, more than men, tend to stress out by mentally reliving their mistakes over and over—heck, it's why stores carry a whole shelf of sleep medications. Cowgirls, on the other hand, shed their mistakes as fast as a dog does its winter coat. When you're riding and ranching, there's no time for dwelling on the past, because you're too busy preparing for the next day. It's important to learn from mistakes before moving on, but don't beat yourself up. It's easier said than done, but shedding your past is critical to rejuvenating your cowgirl spirit. When pity and self-loathing take over, it's hard to find your cowgirl spirit anywhere. Here are some ideas for recharging your cowgirl spirit:

1. Take a cowgirl vacation. Go somewhere that you find relaxing and do what makes you happy. If you're looking for your true western cowgirl spirit, I'd recommend a dude ranch or a drive through old western towns that still reflect the values of a simpler life. Go see where your cowgirl heroes lived and feel what they felt living on the land. You'll find the simplicity of small towns and nature invigorating.

2. Find your giddy-up button. Going through life facing the same-old-things each day is exhausting. It can zap your energy as well as your belief in yourself. Find a project that will give you a great sense of accomplishment and you'll feel your inner drive, shift into high speed. Learn to repel, paint, kayak, or take a master class in cooking. The choice of activity is yours, but pick something you've always wanted to achieve. I've seen women paddle into a rapid looking defeated and come out the other end looking like Sylvester Stallone doing the victory dance in *Rocky II*. BIG accomplishments awaken your cowgirl spirit—all you have to do is go rope one.

3. Quiet your mind. To be honest, I'm still working on this one. It's one of the hardest tasks for overachievers like me. My girlfriends all do yoga and meditate, and you should too. But if you have trouble mastering Zen-like trances, try swimming laps, jogging, listening to music with your eyes closed, or my favorite, spending time in the hot tub. If you don't occasionally quiet your mind, you'll never be able to hear your cowgirl spirit calling.

4. Nurture your mind, body and spirit. It's hard to nurture your spirit if you don't take care of your body. Real cowgirls don't have to workout, but we do. There's no better stress release than exercise, even if it's just taking time each morning to stretch and be thankful for the day ahead.

5. Quit kicking yourself over yesterday. Nothing will come of it except scratched boots and bruised shins. You can't recharge your cowgirl spirit if you're wasting energy worrying over things in the past. To help yourself move forward, make a list of what your mistakes were and ask yourself two important questions: "Was it really my fault?" and "What can I learn from it to make me a better woman?" Complete your analysis, put the paper away, and redirect your energy into more positive thoughts and actions.

17. Die with Your Boots On

Perhaps one of the most important lessons I learned from cowgirls, both past and present, is to greet aging head-on and see it as the ultimate challenge. When a horse grows old, you put it out to pasture. Some horses learn to wile away the days eating grass, but others neigh at the gate each morning, because they still want to come along. I've rarely heard of a cowgirl who doesn't stand ready to ride each day, even when her body is telling her otherwise. Many a son or daughter has learned the hard way that you can't retire a cowgirl before she's ready. That's a battle you will not win.

Cowgirls in the Old West had a knack for living well beyond their fragile eastern sisters. Out on the range, working hard from sun up to sundown and rarely a doctor for miles, they beat the actuarial odds over and over again. "Why was that?" I kept wondering. Sure there were many women out West who died young giving birth, but I found the hardworking cowgirl, muscular and fit, was more likely to round-up cattle in the morning, give birth in the afternoon, and have dinner waiting for her cowhands. The fact is, these women were tough. They weren't going to let something like childbirth or old age slow them down. But the other factor which played an enormous role was their unbridled attitude toward life. They couldn't wait to see what the next day would bring. Boredom wasn't in their vocabulary. To say they were optimistic wouldn't cover the gamut of their outlook on life.

Adopting this passion for living can truly make you cowgirl smart. Not only will you live longer, but you'll enjoy all the days of your life. Below are some short glimpses at several cowgirls who never quit riding and were proud to die with their boots on.

Probably one of my favorite centurion cowgirls was Connie Reeves, who is best known for her motto, "Always saddle your own horse." But for those who knew Connie, she was better known for proving that aging doesn't have to slow you down. Connie died at 101 years-of-age with her boots on after being thrown from her favorite horse, Dr. Pepper. News of her death was carried in newspapers across the United States, but not in the obituary section; the articles weren't a statement of her death, but more a celebration of her long life. Major papers like *The New York Times, The Boston Globe, The Dallas Morning News* and *USA Today*, eulogized this unknown cowgirl as if she was a dignitary. She was a simple cowgirl, living a simple life, teaching young girls to ride. However, her attitude and the vigor for which she approached life were anything but ordinary and made her life story astounding.

The same month in which she died, Connie was still working on speeches that she was scheduled to give. She had plans for several trips with friends. She was still visiting the Waldemar

Camp stables as often as her schedule allowed, overseeing campers' riding lessons. At 101, she had no plans for slowing down. Her passion for life was amazing, and when her story appeared in 2003, it made women everywhere aspire to be cowgirl smart at a ripe old age, just like Connie Reeves.

Like Connie, Fern Sawyer also lived for the day, but she did so at a much faster speed. Fern embodied the full-throttle lifestyle of an action-packed cowgirl. She was unstoppable and unflappable, whether it was ranching, rodeoing or politicking. She had quite a sassy attitude and she wasn't afraid to share it.

Fern was the first woman to win the cutting horse championship at the Fort Worth Fat Stock Show and Rodeo in 1945—a feat not equaled by any woman for over four decades—and she competed in almost every rodeo event in the 1930s and 1940s. In the late 1940s, when they stopped letting women compete in most rodeo events, Fern embraced the idea of the first "all-girl rodeo," as it was originally called. At thirty years old, she competed and won almost every event, including all-round cowgirl.

In 1946, Fern was one of the founding members of the National Cutting Horse Association. It was an all-male group, and Fern pushed hard to make them let her in. Now this may not seem like such a big achievement unless you consider that clubs like Rotary International didn't allow women members until the 1980s. A year after breaking into the men's club of cutting,

Fern beat out 150 men to win the Association's National Cutting Horse Championship—the only event where men and women still compete head-to-head. Fern never let a little thing like gender slow her down, but she also never worried with being a woman's libber; she fiercely fought that label.

With an enormous closet full of custom boots and chic western wear, Fern was known as a flashy dresser even into her seventies. She typically topped-off her attire with buckles the size of dinner plates. Feisty would be too gentle a word to describe Fern. Her tough cowgirl talk was as bold as her wardrobe, and she unleashed it best in New Mexico politics where she was a staunch democrat. Later in life, she became an outspoken rodeo judge and proponent for women in rodeo. While some thought her cowgirl verve was too bold, there was no doubt she could back up her bravado with enough championship saddles, buckles, trophies and Hall of Fame plaques to cover an entire room in her house. After all, it was her talent—not her fashion—that earned her a place in the Cutting Horse, Cowboy and Cowgirl Halls of Fame.

Fern had a great philosophy of life, "Do all you can as fast as you can." She lived life in the fast lane and refused to take up golf at sixty-two, because it was too slow. In her sixties, Fern told Teresa Jordan, author of the book *Cowgirls: Women of the American West:*

I'm real lucky, I guess. I'm real healthy.

For my age, I feel like I'm pretty young. I try to keep my body in real good shape. If you're roping and riding and skiing and playing tennis at my age, you have to be healthy. They say it's all down hill from here, but I never think of that. I'm always looking for tomorrow…I'm always going to have a good time. I have never been bored in my life.

At seventy-six, Fern arrived wearing stretch pants and a gold leather jacket to film a PBS special about her life. The PBS special, titled "Just for the Ride," covered Fern's cowgirl career as well as her bodacious lifestyle. One of the opening scenes showed Fern in her latest Cadillac and discussed her love of fast cars. It seems Fern made Jan & Dean's "Little Old Lady from Pasadena" look like milk toast.

Fern died of a heart attack on horseback while filming the PBS show in 1993. Fern lived BIG until the day she died. Some say her days were cut short, but Fern would have been proud that she died with her boots on doing what she loved—riding in the spotlight. She was a heavy smoker and a hard drinker, so seventy-six was probably longer than most friends expected her to live. Fern attributed her health and longevity to working on her ranch. She claimed that people who didn't work or who had too much idle time were in bad shape—both mentally and physically. I'd say her reasoning was just plain cowgirl smart.

There are plenty of senior cowgirls still roping and riding today. They even have Senior Pro Rodeos and the National Senior Pro Rodeo Finals, sponsored by the National Old Timers Rodeo Association (check out SeniorRodeo.com for their amazing stories). Each year, more than a dozen women over sixty compete for all-round cowgirl. They are positively inspiring.

Dora Rhoads Waldrop, a Cowgirl Hall of Fame inductee, celebrated her seventy-sixth birthday barrel racing at the 1987 Living Legends Rodeo in Canadian, Texas. That same year, she earned the All-Around High Point trophy from the Texas Quarter Horse Association. Only a year later, at seventy-seven, she was barred from competing because of her age. She urged friends to take up a letter-writing campaign to allow her entry. "You are never a quitter," Dora said, "until you quit trying." Darn right Dora! You go girl!

Lessons Learned

My cowgirl heroes have convinced me that I want to be an outrageous old woman that is never accused of being an old lady. I want to keep following my passion until I disintegrate from the power of sheer joy. The number of years I live is not as important as whether or not I've lived them fully. For regardless of my age or time of my death, I want to die with my boots on. How about you? Have the cowgirls in this book inspired you to rope a more kick-ass life even into your senior years? If so, below are a few tips to make the trail ride between here and your 100th birthday, the trip you've always wanted.

1. Die with your boots on. It means you never stop riding or doing the things you love. Cowgirls don't give up on life and you shouldn't either. Have high expectations for your senior years and make them a reality by exercising often and staying in good shape. You'll need a youthful body if you're to keep up with your young-minded plans. Keep exercising your mind as well since you'll need to outsmart all those wet-behind-the-ear, whippersnappers on your ninetieth birthday. Being cowgirl smart takes stamina and brains.

2. Stay fulfilled. Most women are surprised that staying fulfilled requires a little work. Fulfillment doesn't come to you like a dream, you have to reach out and try new things. Focusing all your time on your kids or sitting by the pool may seem fulfilling today, but I can guarantee you, neither will last. With time comes change, and you'll need to be ready. It's another scenario where life is like riding: each time you change direction on a horse, you need to change the lead. Life is no different, and if you'll find your new lead with each change in life, you'll find the ride a lot more entertaining.

3. Work hard. One of the two reasons Wild

West cowgirls typically lived longer than their city-slicker sisters was manual labor and an undying optimism. You might think the two are incompatible, but that isn't true for cowgirls. They worked hard at what they loved. Don't shy from hard work, for there's no such thing as "women's work." Put your strength behind something you love, whether it's work or a hobby. Don't think of your retirement job as being a couch potato—start a new career you've always wanted to try. No matter what your age, hard work will make life more rewarding.

4. Work hard, play hard. This is my second favorite motto in life and it should be one of your favorites, too. Hard work is fine and good, but balance that with some unbridled playtime. We all love playtime, but many women don't allow themselves to indulge in it. It can be as simple as an evening laughing with girlfriends or as elaborate as attending a ball for your favorite charity. Whatever your choice, learn to play hard.

Warning: Too Much Cowgirl Smarts Can Be Too Much

Following the Cowgirl Creed is a sure way to become cowgirl smart, but it's also possible to get too much of a good thing. For example, if you kick up too much dust by bucking all the rules, you might find yourself riding alone, simply because you're too much trouble to travel with. It's just as important to know the difference between dreaming big and having unrealistic goals. Even facing your fears can be taken too far if you become reckless with your life. Being cowgirl smart requires that you know the difference between being confident, assertive and determined versus being arrogant, overbearing and obstinate. It's a fine line that can be easily crossed when you're hell-bent on getting there.

Calamity Jane is the perfect example of a cowgirl with too much smarts for her own good. She bucked the rules alright, but she took it to the extreme, making herself infamous rather than famous. She might have been one of the bravest sure shots in the West, but she lost the respect of others by also being the roughest, crudest cowhand in the saloon. For all her cowgirl smarts, Calamity always found herself drunk, broke and alone.

Belle Star and her outlaw girlfriends are also good examples of taking cowgirls smarts too far. Belle began by being an audacious, self-empowered woman, but she let it go to her head. In her mind, the sun came up just to hear her crow. She used her feminine wiles to get out of jail so many times that she came to believe that she was above the law. But her days of riding high in the saddle came to an end when one man tired of her arrogant cowgirl ways and shot her in the back.

I've seen my share of modern cowgirls who overdosed on cowgirl smarts, too. Two cow gals from up North I once worked with were two of the smartest, most creative Web designers I'd ever met. Self-taught and ambitious, they were burning up the Internet. Unfortunately, they were so obstinate, that they wouldn't have moved their camp for a prairie fire. Even though they were unbelievably skilled, they were continually surprised when their customers never hired them again. When cowgirls refuse to take instruction or advice from friends or clients, they're not using their cowgirl smarts.

One cowgirl I met on a roundup in Texas was constantly telling everyone how to saddle, where to set their stirrups, how to track the strays, when to charge the longhorns and where to hold the line. She wasn't the trail boss, she just thought she was. She might have been balanced in the saddle, but she couldn't balance her helpfulness with being a good hand. When we stopped for breaks and dismounted our tired steeds, I noticed she never climbed down from her high horse, figuratively or literally. Later, I found out why: she couldn't lift herself up into the saddle without a mounting block and no one offered to give her a leg up. Despite all her cowboying advice, she couldn't even get on the horse. Before you start showing the world how much cowgirl smarts you have, be sure you're able to do for yourself.

When adopting your own cowgirl smarts, be sure to remember that too much of a good thing definitely can be too much.

Best of Luck

I hope these cowgirl stories have inspired you to rope a more kick-ass life.

Ellen Reid Smith

About The Author

Ellen Reid Smith has been in awe of cowgirls most of her life. As one of the youngest female executives at American Airlines and IBM focused on customer loyalty in global businesses, she had few female mentors, so she modeled herself after the strongest women she knew—cowgirls who settled the Wild West. She believes that a cowgirl spirit is a state of mind that makes cowgirls in the boardroom just as commonplace as on a ranch.

Ellen runs a consulting practice in customer loyalty marketing (www.ReidSmith. com) serving Fortune 500 companies. She has presented customer loyalty seminars on four continents and authored the first business book on e-loyalty which was published in nine languages. She lives in Texas and Colorado where she and her pardner Josef ride their two favorite horses, Stetson and Happy.

Ellen is also the author of The Cowgirl Smarts Coloring Book that teaches The Cowgirl Creed to little buckaroos. Other books coming out soon in the Cowgirl Smarts series include: Cowgirl Smarts: How to Kick-Ass in Business, Cowgirl Smarts for Teens and "Cowgirl Smarts Travel: A Guide to Finding Your Cowgirl Spirit." To buy other Cowgirl Smarts books and merchandise go to www.cowgirlsmarts.com.

Have Ellen Reid Smith Speak at Your Event

Ellen Reid Smith's Cowgirl Smarts presentations are great for adults, teens and business leaders alike. She applies her cowgirl point of view to three subject areas: how to rope more out of life life; how women can succeed in business; and how to improve customer loyalty. She mixes bodacious cowgirl tales with real life and real business examples to make learning fun. And because Ellen has a proven track record in both corporate and entreprenuerial business, is internationally known as a customer loyalty guru and still manages to find time to rope her own kick-ass life, audiences find her message compelling.

She uses cowgirl wit to relay how Wild West herioines are some of the best role models for the 21st Century whether you're a student, stay-at-home mom, entreprenuer or corporate exectutive. Wether she Cowgirl Smarts life or business, she keeps audiences laughing, thinking and ready to make positive changes. Her most popular presentations include:

1. Cowgirl Smarts: How to Rope A Kick-Ass Life
2. Cowgirl Smarts for Teens
3. Cowgirl Habits of Highly Successful Women
4. Finding Your Cowgirl Spirit and Passing it on to Your Children

5. Management Lessons From a Trailboss
6. How Cowgirls Kick-Ass in Business
7. Cowgirl Ethics Applied to Business
8. Ride for the Brand: How to Improve Employee Loyalty
9. How Your Company Can Use Cowgirl Smarts to Improve Customer Loyalty
10. Management Secrets I Learned From My Horse

If you'd like to have Ellen speak at your next event, visit www.CowgirlSmarts.com for a full list of presentations and descriptions, or call the Cowgirl Smarts Headquarters at 512-301-7223.

Bibliography by Chapter

1. Dare to be a cowgirl

Duncan, Roberta S., "Elizabeth Ellen (Lizzie) Johnson Williams," *The Handbook of Texas Online*

Shelton, Emily Jones, "Lizzie E. Johnson: A Cattle Queen of Texas," *Southwestern Historical Quarterly* (January 1947), pp. 355-62.

2. Buck the rules

Crosby, Thelma, and Eve Ball, Bob Crosby, *World Champion Cowboy*, (Clarendon, Texas: Clarendon Press, 1966), pp. 156-157

Warren Richardson, "History of First Frontier Days Celebration," *Annals of Wyoming* (Wyoming: 1947), pp. 42-43.

3. Stay balanced in the saddle

Hull, Robert Charlton, *The Search for Adele Parker*, Libra Publishers, Inc. (Roslyn Heights, New York, 1974).

Hull, Robert Charlton, "Adele Von Ohl Parker: Something of a Gypsy." Sunday Magazine, *The Plain Dealer*, November 4, 1973 (Cleveland, Ohio).

Beautiful, Daring Western Girls: Women of the Wild West Shows, Exhibit guide at the Buffalo Bill Historical Center. (Cody, Wyoming, 1985, 1991)

4. Ride the trail of adventure

Hunter, Marvin J., ed., *The Trail Drivers of Texas*. Nashville, (Tennessee: Cokesbury Press, 1925).

5. Dream as big as Texas

"A Daring Western Woman: Texas Girl Who Acts as Cattle Guard," *Denver Times,* (February 17, 1901).

Kerttula, T.H, "There Was No Christmas," *True West* (December 1963).

6. Be tough, but be feminine

Wallis, Michael, *The Real Wild West, The 101 Ranch and the Creation of the American West*, (New York, New York; St. Martin's Press, 1999).

Savage, Candace, *Cowgirls*. (Berkeley, California: Ten Speed Press, 1996).

Roach, Joyce Gibson, *The Cowgirls*, (Denton, Texas: University of North Texas Press, 1990).

7. Attack life like it's a 1,000 lb. steer

LeCompte, Mary Lou, *Cowgirls of the Rodeo: Pioneer Professional Athletes*. (Chicago, Illinois: University of Illinois Press, 1993).

Risk, Milt, Those Magnificent Cowgirls: A History of the Rodeo Cowgirl. (Cheyenne, Wyoming: Wyoming Publishing, 1983).

Savage, Candace, *Cowgirls*. (Berkeley, California: Ten Speed Press, 1996).

Wills, Kathy Lynn and Virginia Artho, *Cowgirl Legends From the Cowgirl Hall of Fame.* (Salt Lake City, Utah: Gibbs-Smith Publishing, 1995).

8. Saddle your own horse
Reeves, Connie, *I Married a Cowboy*, (Austin, Texas: Eakin Press, 1995).
Reid Smith, Ellen "Cowgirl Smarts: How to Rope Yourself a Kick-Ass Life," *Brilliant,* April 2004, p. 88-89.

9. Rein in your fears
Collins, Elizabeth Smith, Ed. by Alvin E. Dyer, *The Cattle Queen of Montana* (Spokane: Dyer Printing Company, 2nd edition of 1898 or 1902? self-published biography)
Greenough, Alice, "What a Cowgirl Wants From Life," *Physical Culture: The Personal Problem Magazine,* May 1937, pp. 50-51.
Jordan, Teresa, *Cowgirls, Women of the American West* (Garden City, New York: Anchor Books/Doubleday, 1984).
"Meet the Cowgirl," *The New York Woman Magazine*, January 1937.

10. Dress for success—the cowgirl way
Boatright, Moody C., "The American Rodeo," *American Quarterly*, Summer 1964, p. 202.

11. Ride high in the saddle
Stewart, Elinore Pruitt, *Letters of a Woman Homesteader*, (New York, New York:

Houghton Mifflin 1988, original copyright
1913).

12. Ride high, but stay grounded
Smith, Ellen Reid, Interview with Helen
    Groves at the National Cowgirl Museum
    and Hall of Fame on April 1, 2003.

13. Give others a leg up
Roach, Joyce Gibson, *The Cowgirls*, (Denton,
    Texas: Univerrsity of North Texas Press,
    1990).
Risk, Milt, *Those Magnificent Cowgirls*, (Wyo-
    ming: Wyoming Publishing, 1983).

14. Always get back on the horse
Mosley, Ruby, "I'm a Cowgirl," *Range Lore
    Volume*, Federal Writers Project, Library of
    Congress (San Angelo, Texas: 1935 inter-
    view date).
Joan Burbick, *Rodeo Queens and the Ameri-
    can Dream*, pages 31-32, (New York, New
    York: Public Affairs 2002).

15. Ride beside your man
Doyle, "Mrs. Jack Miles," *Range Lore*, The
    Federal Writers Project (San Angelo, Texas:
    1941)
Riley, Glenda, "Annie Oakley Creating the
    Cowgirl," *Montana The Magazine of West-
    ern History*. Vol. 45, #3, Summer 1995, pp.
    32-47.
Wallis, Michael, *The Real Wild West, The 101*

Ranch and the Creation of the American West, (New York, New York; St. Martin's Press, 1999).

16. Recharge your cowgirl spirit

Ehrlich, Gretel, *The Solace of Open Spaces*. (New York, New York: Penguin Press, 1985).

Stillwell, Hallie Crawford, *I'll Gather My Geese* (College Station, Texas: Texas A&M University Press, 1991).

17. Die with your boots on

Jordan, Teresa, *Cowgirls, Women of the American West* (Garden City, New York: Anchor Books/Doubleday, 1984).

Wills, Kathy Lynn and Virginia Artho, *Cowgirl Legends from the Cowgirl Hall of Fame* (Salt Lake City, Utah: Gibbs-Smith Publisher, 1995).